ZenDooDle GALORE

Advanced Coloring Book

The Creativity Tree

Golden Rocket Publishing

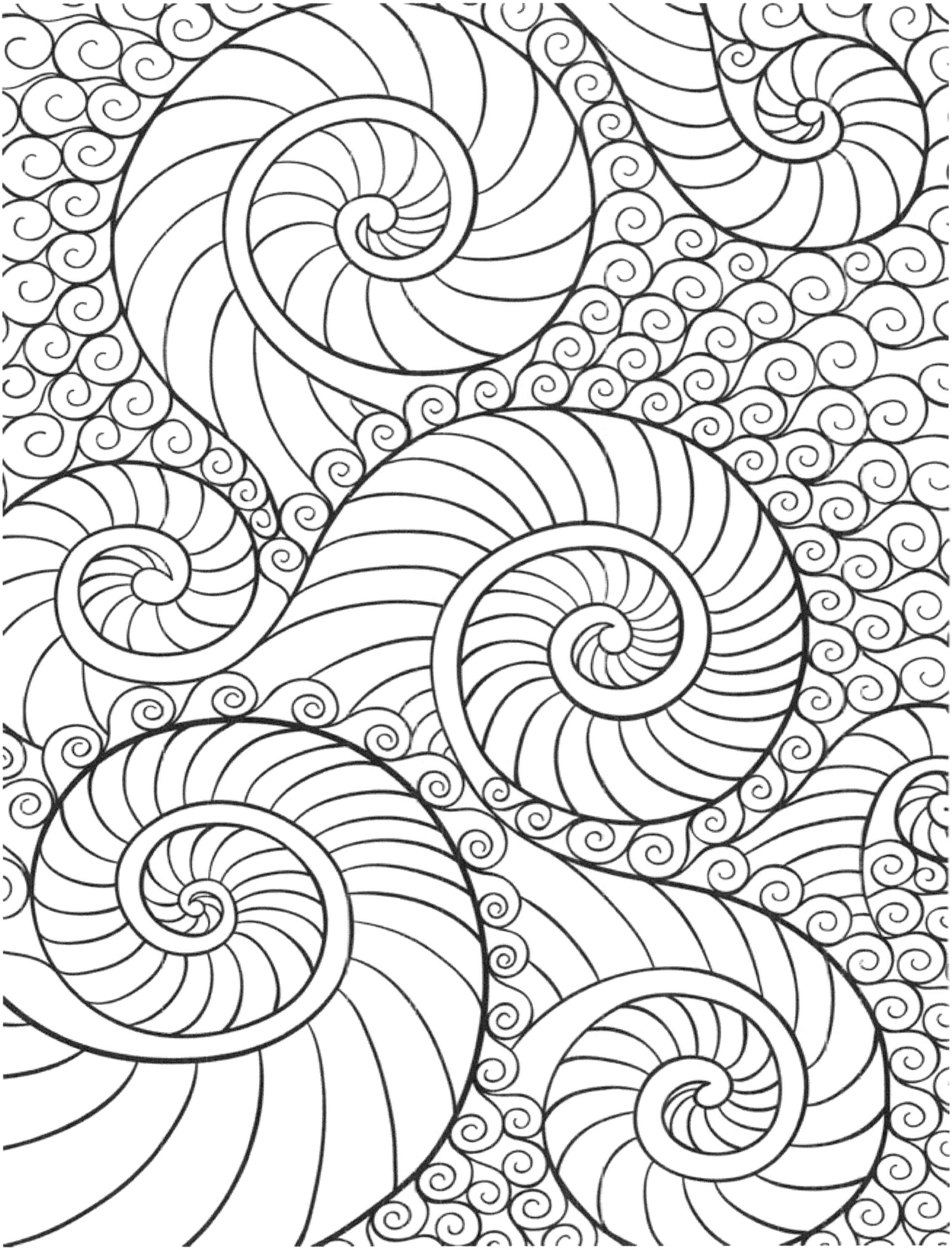

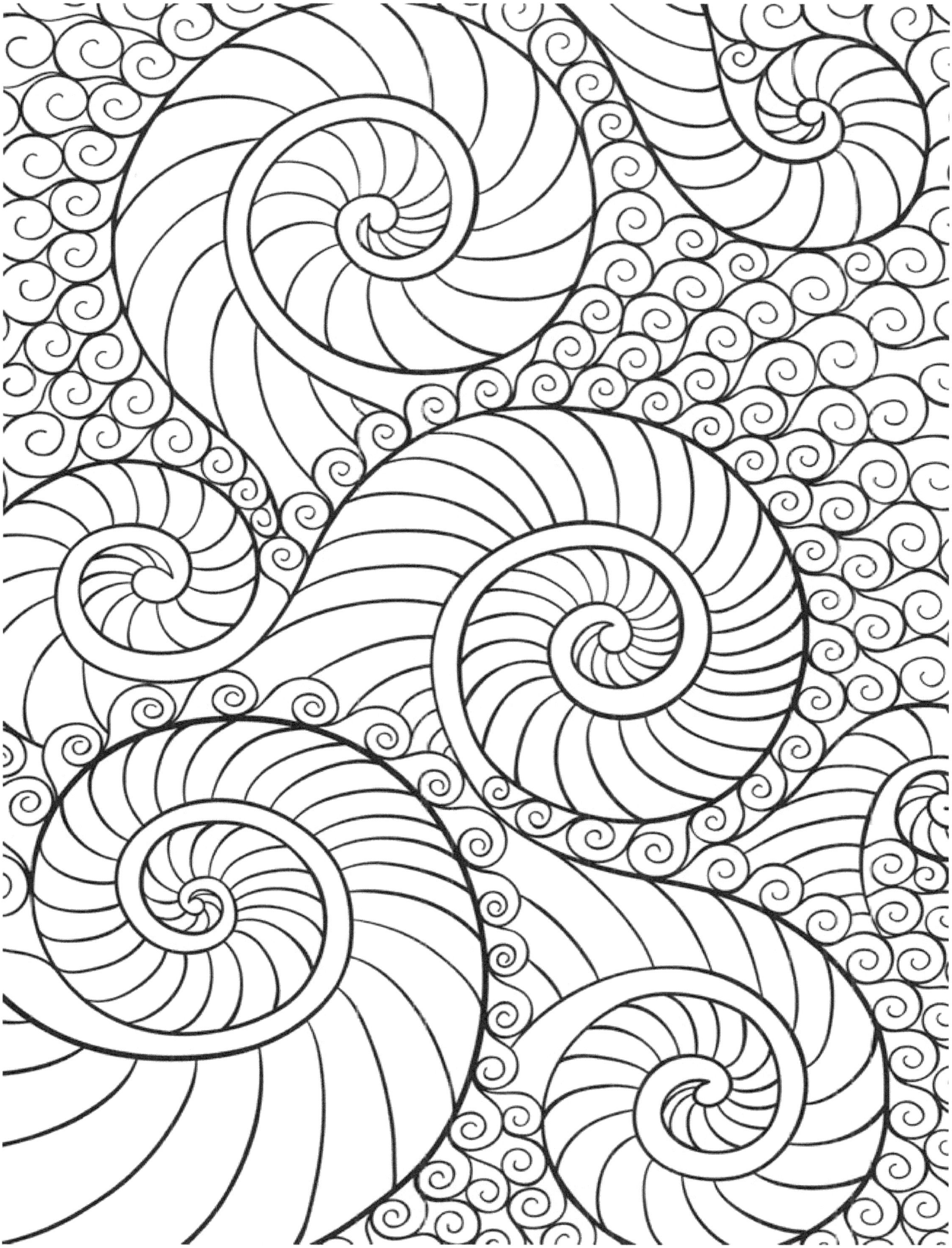

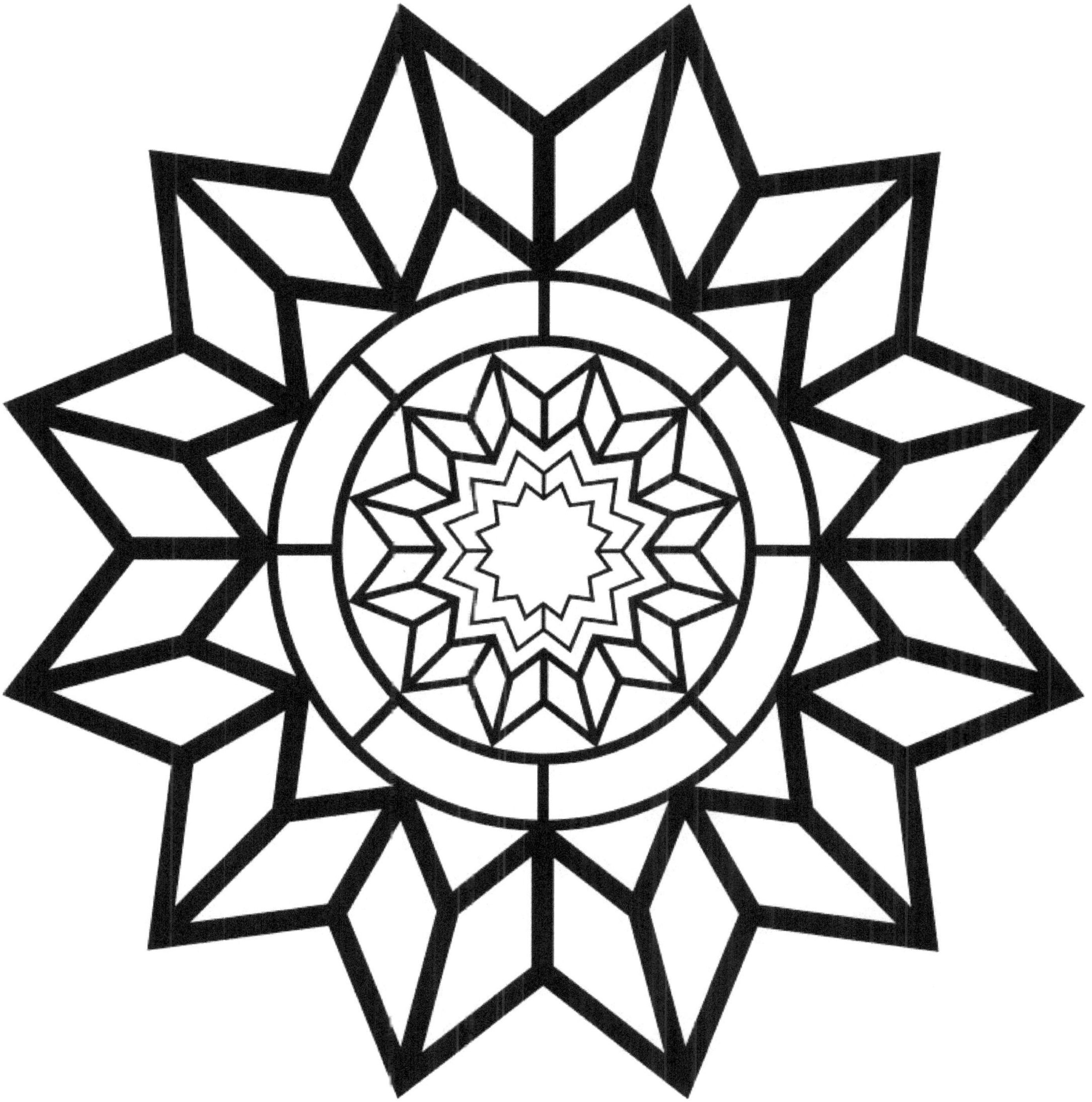

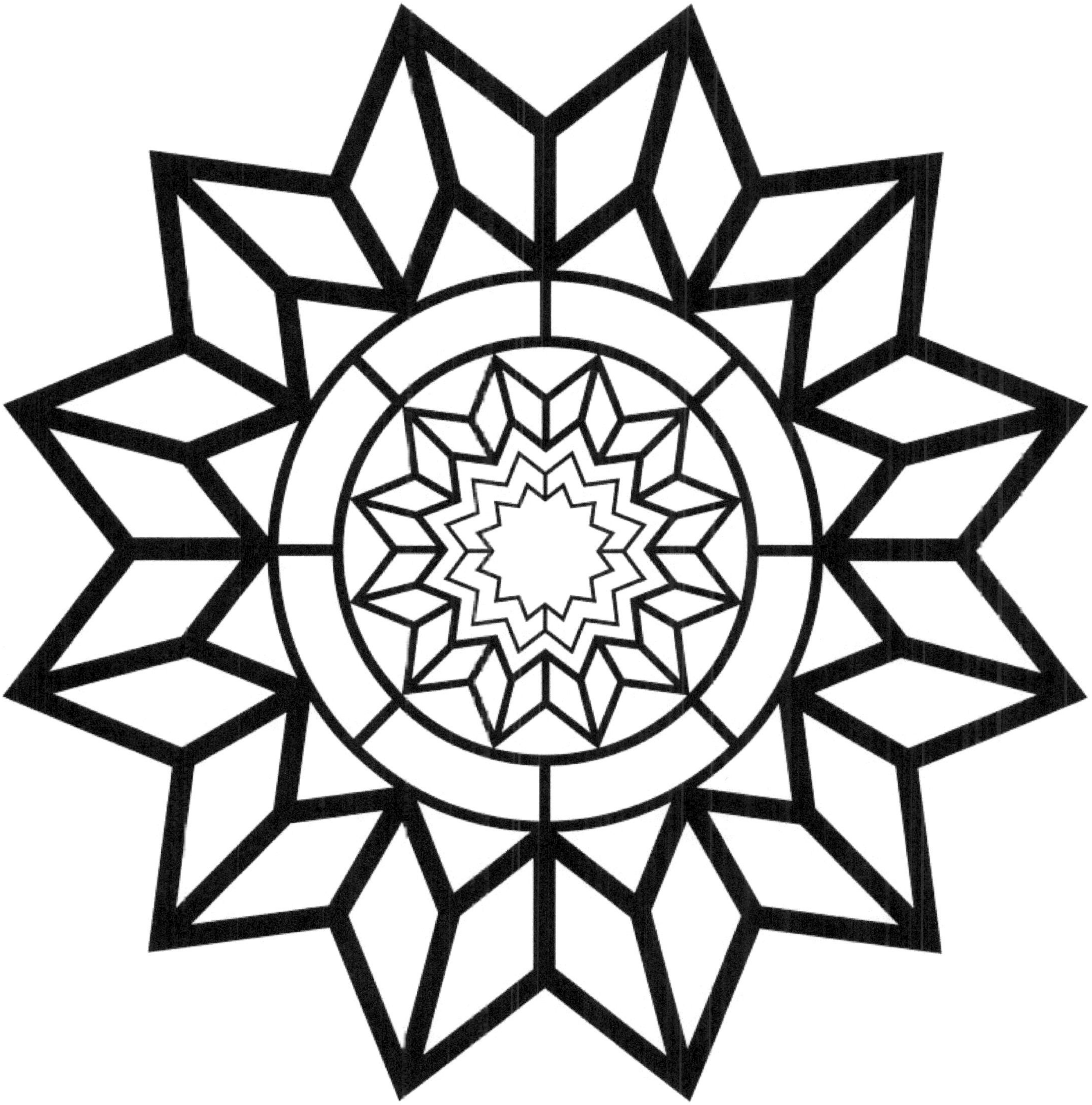

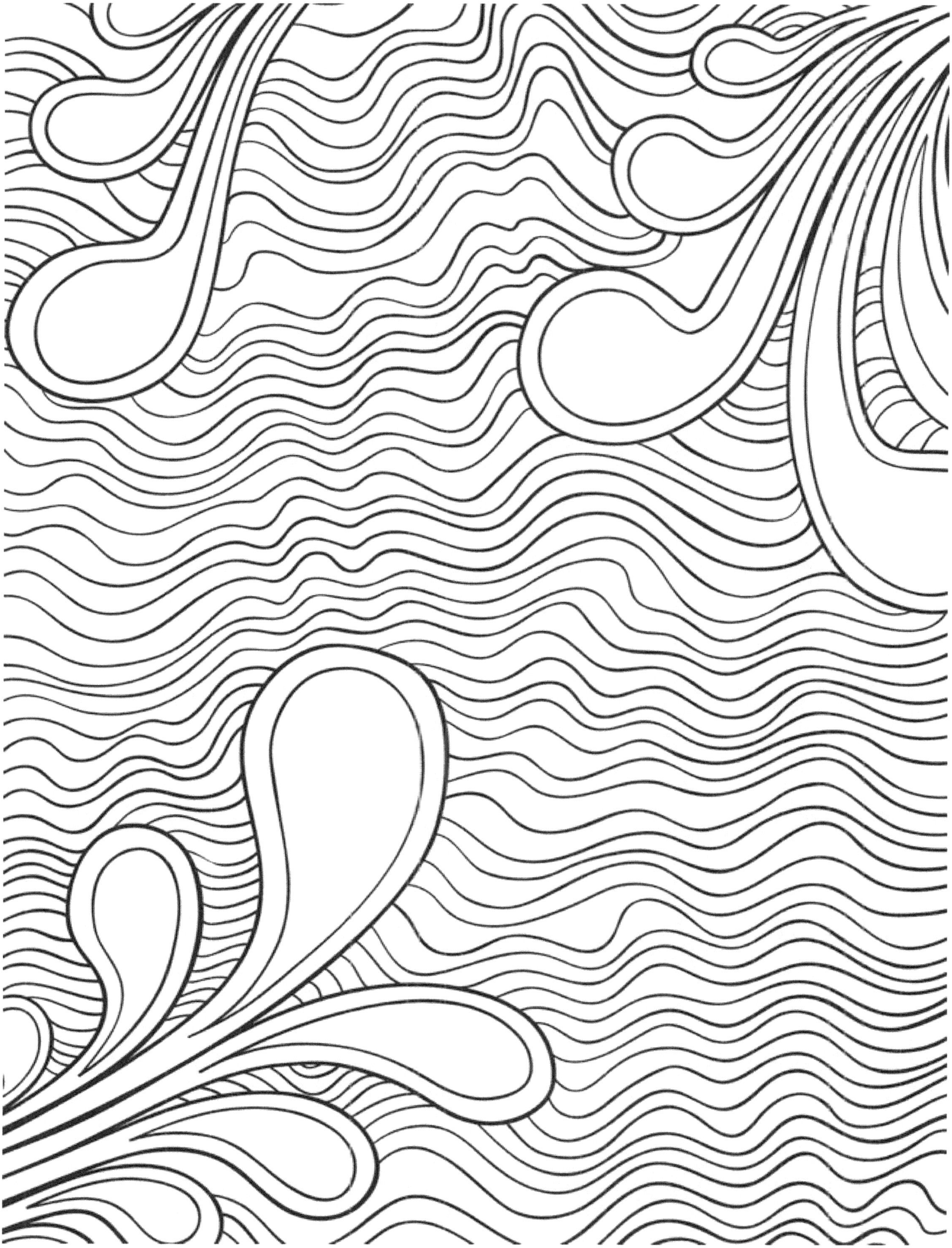

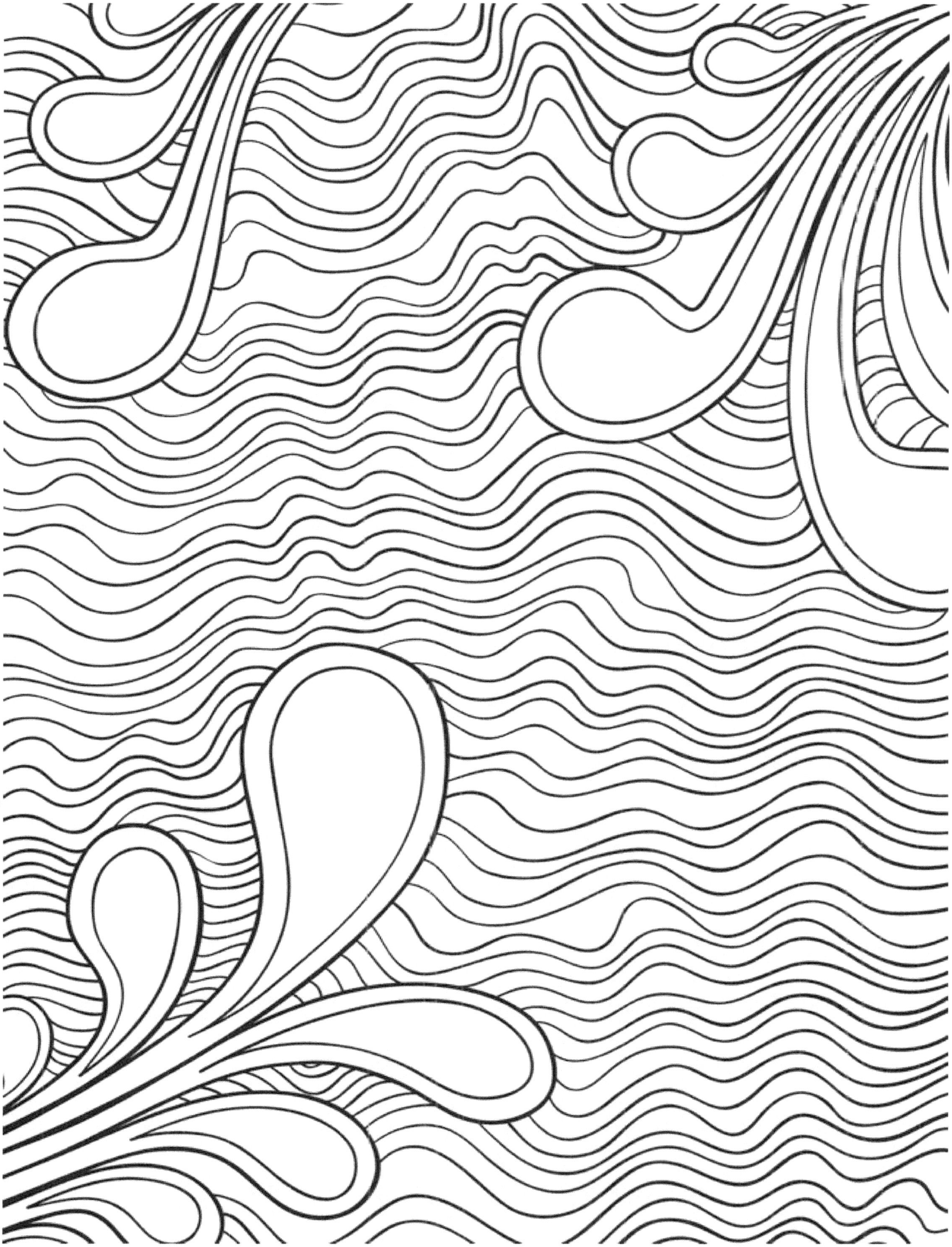

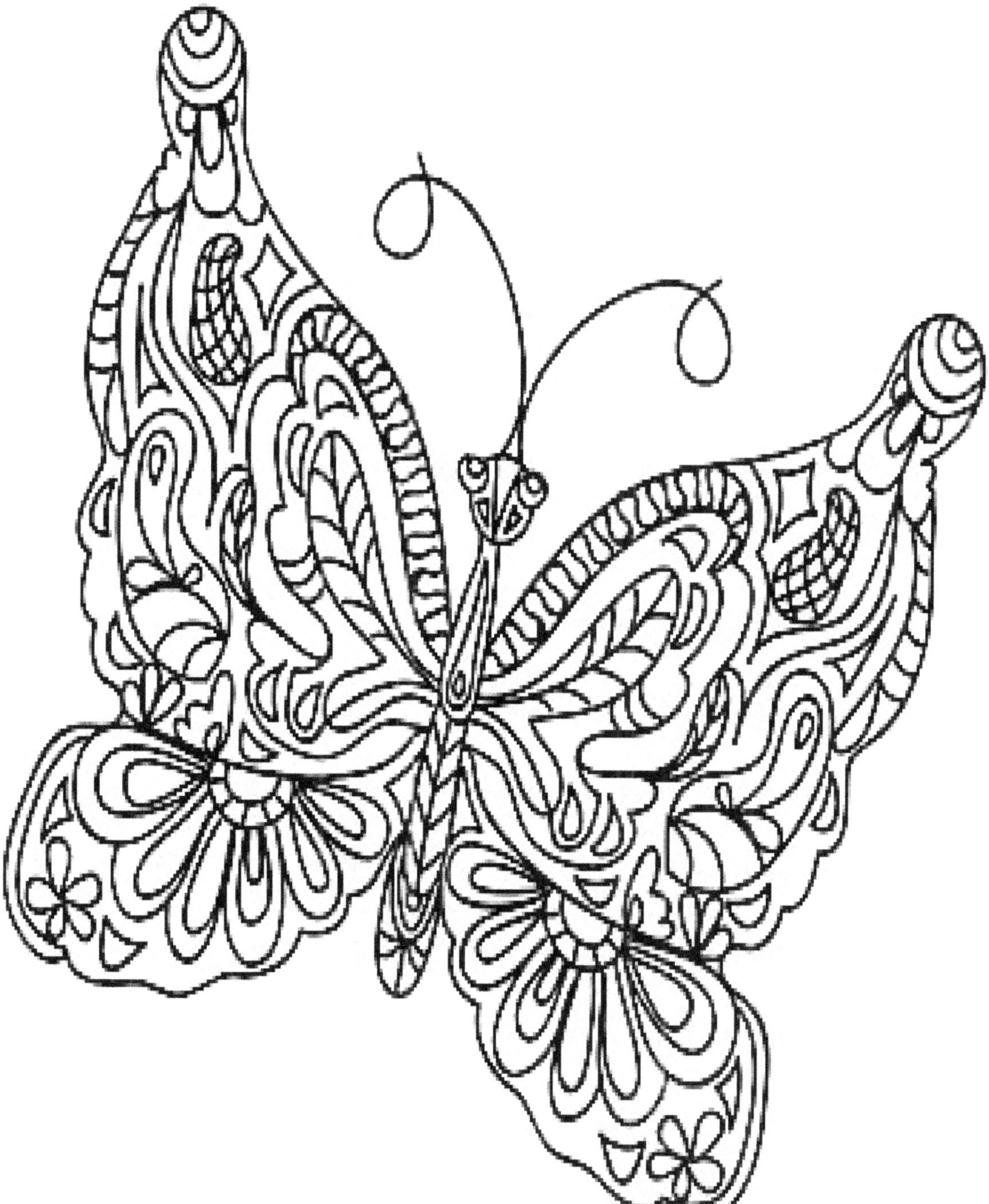

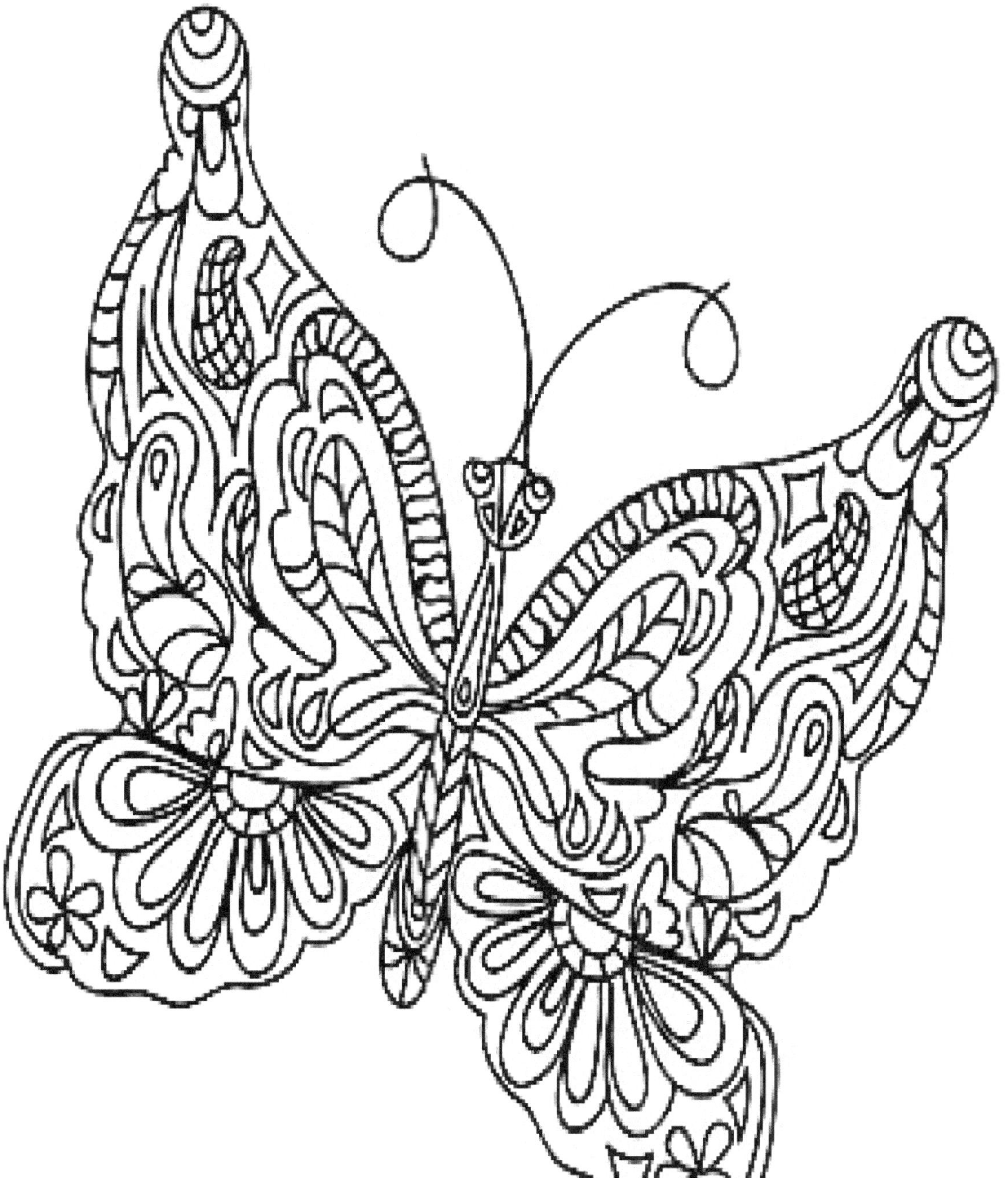

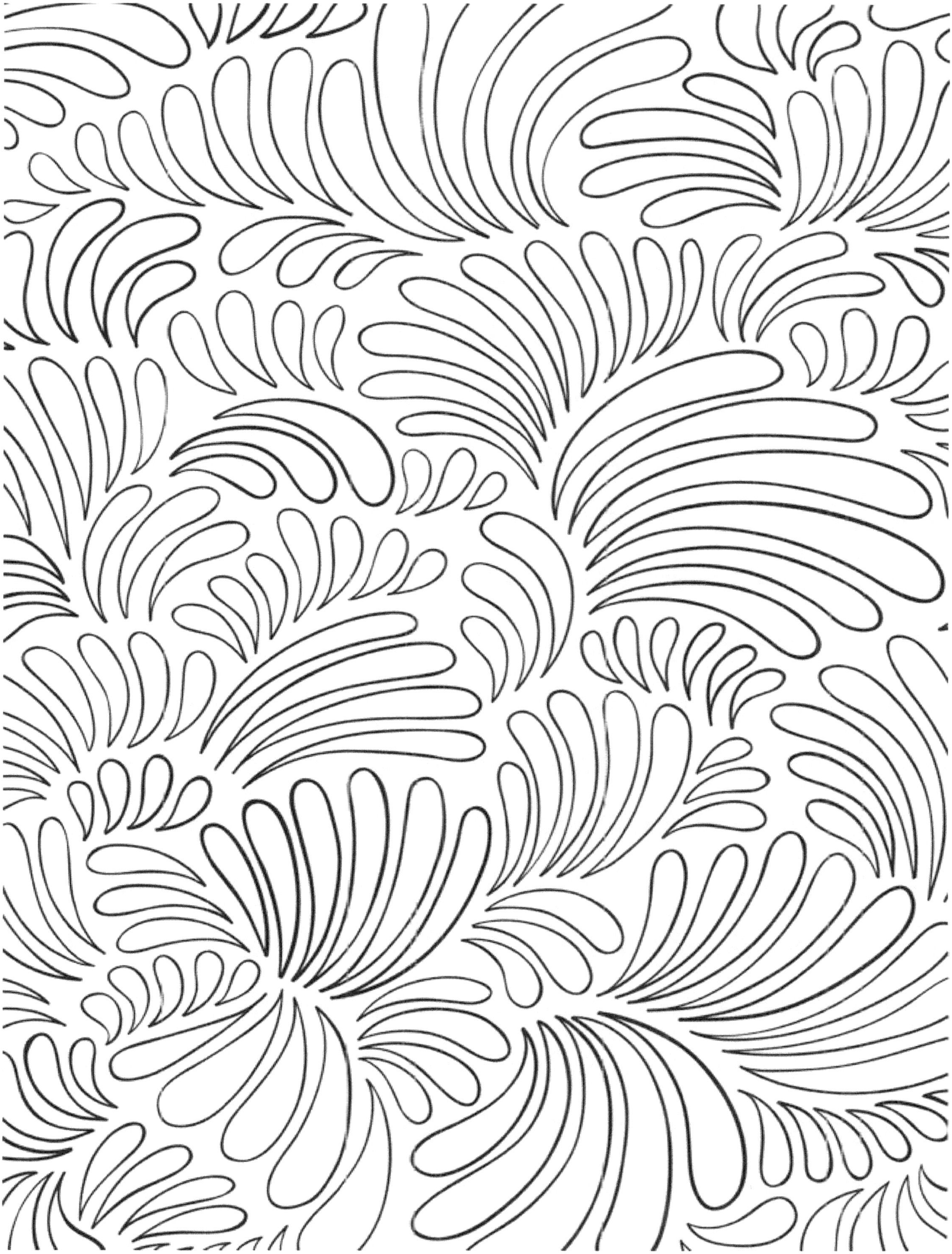

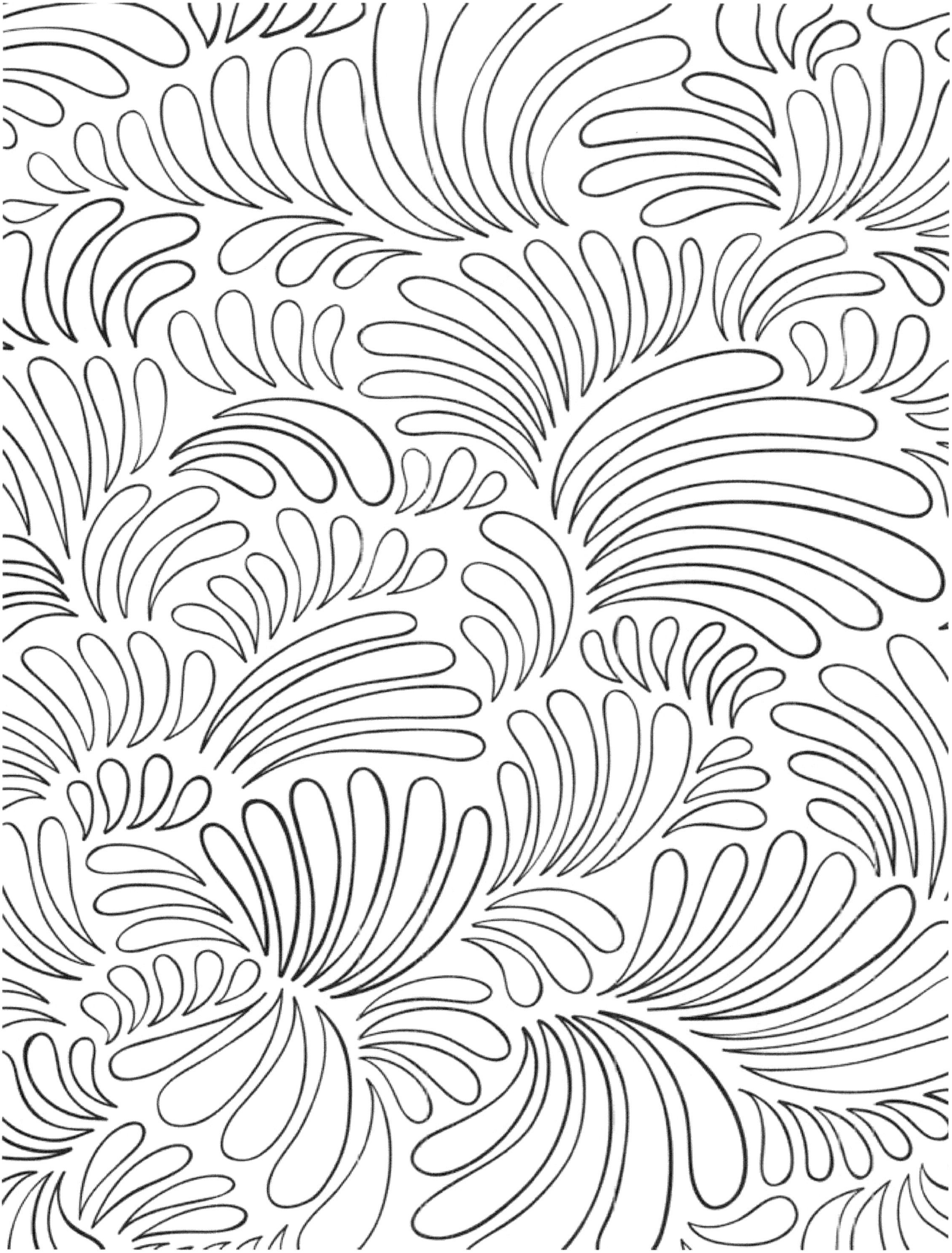

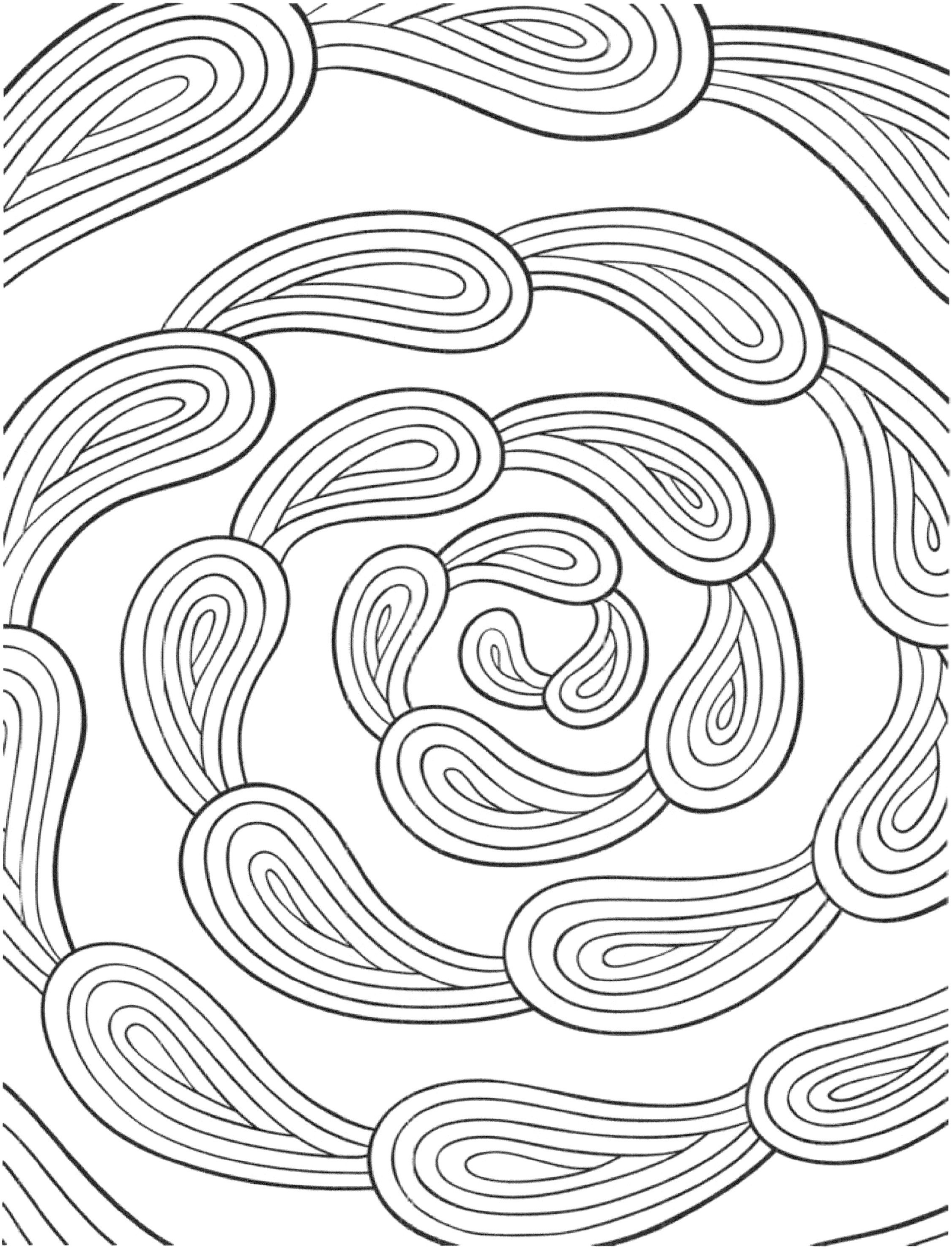

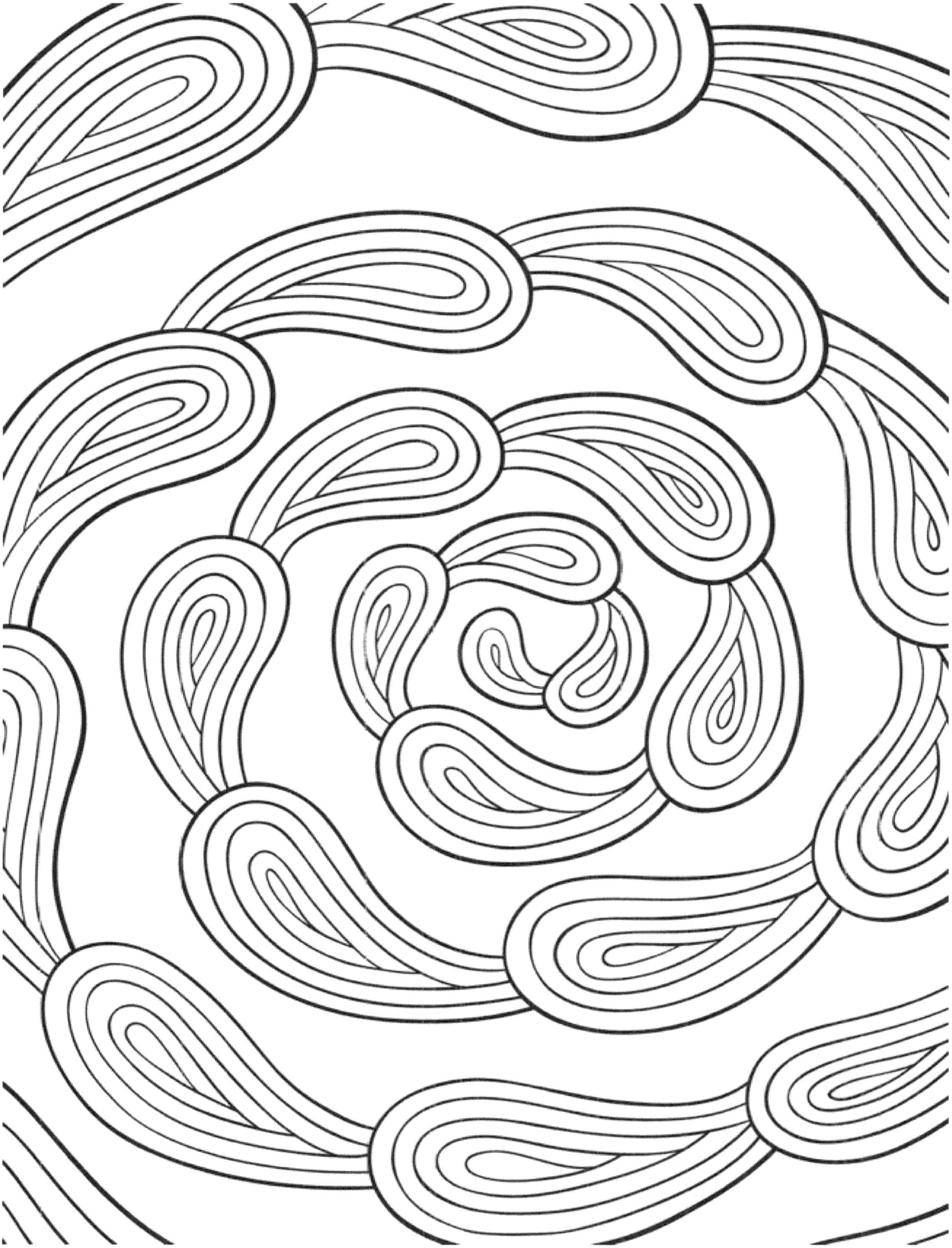

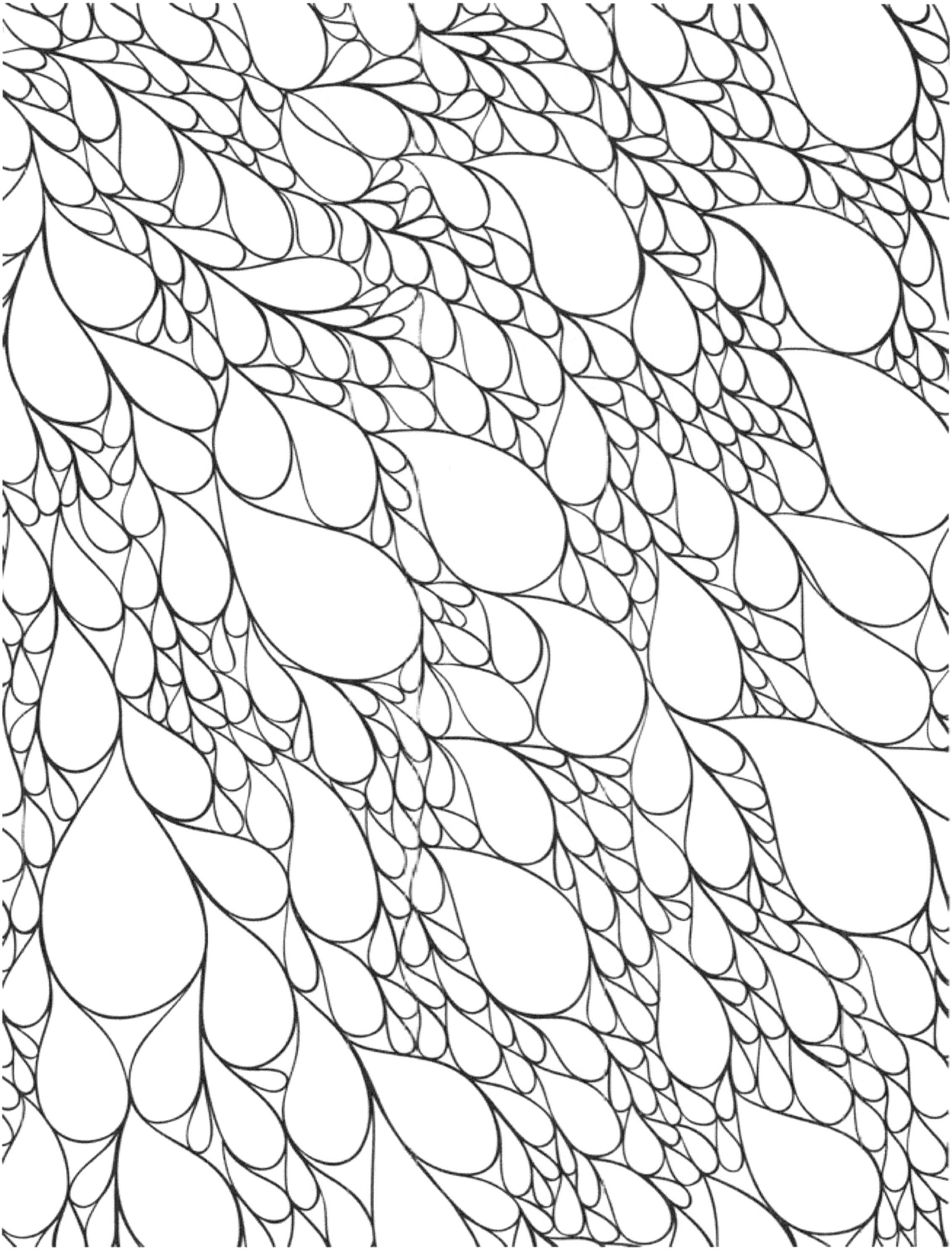

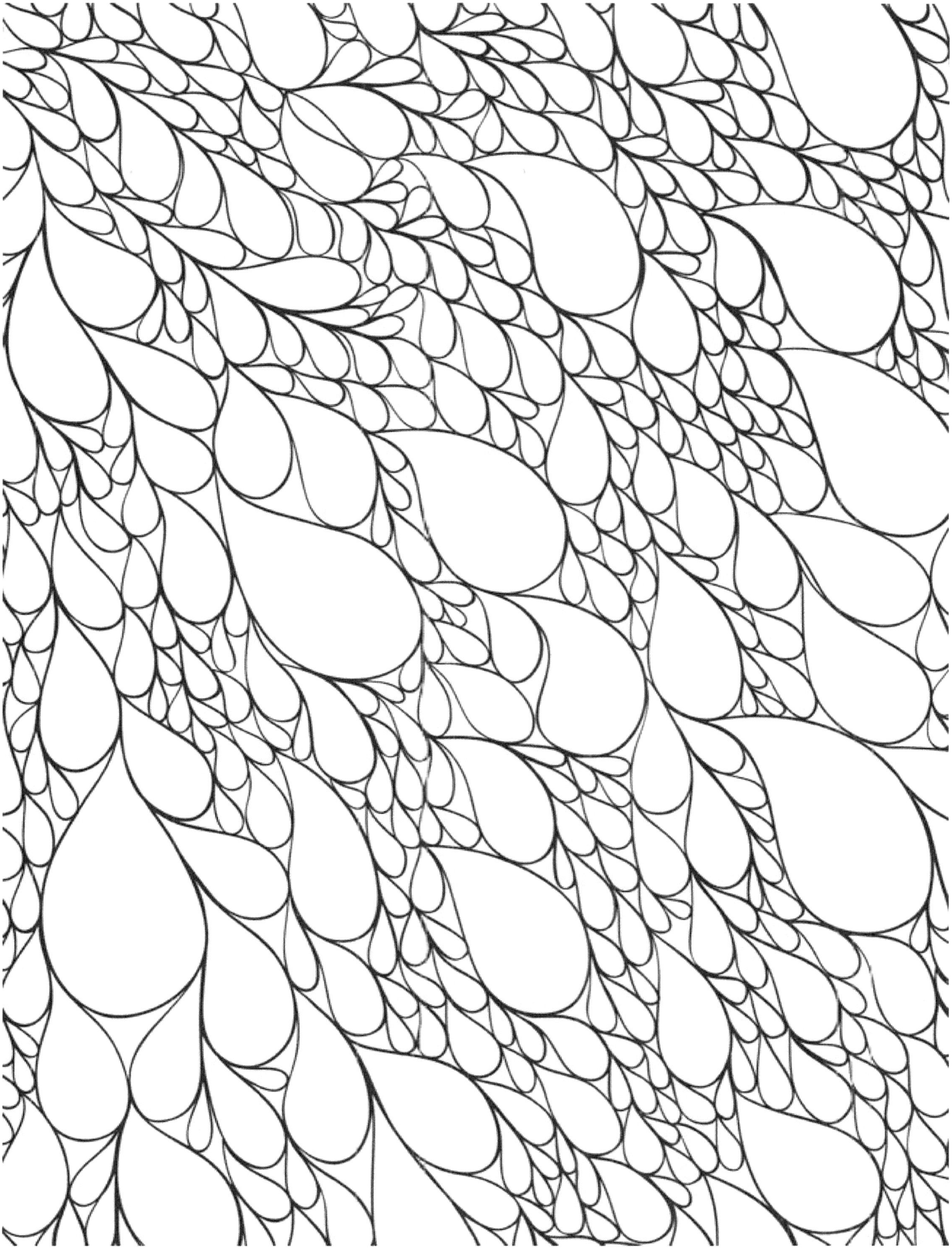

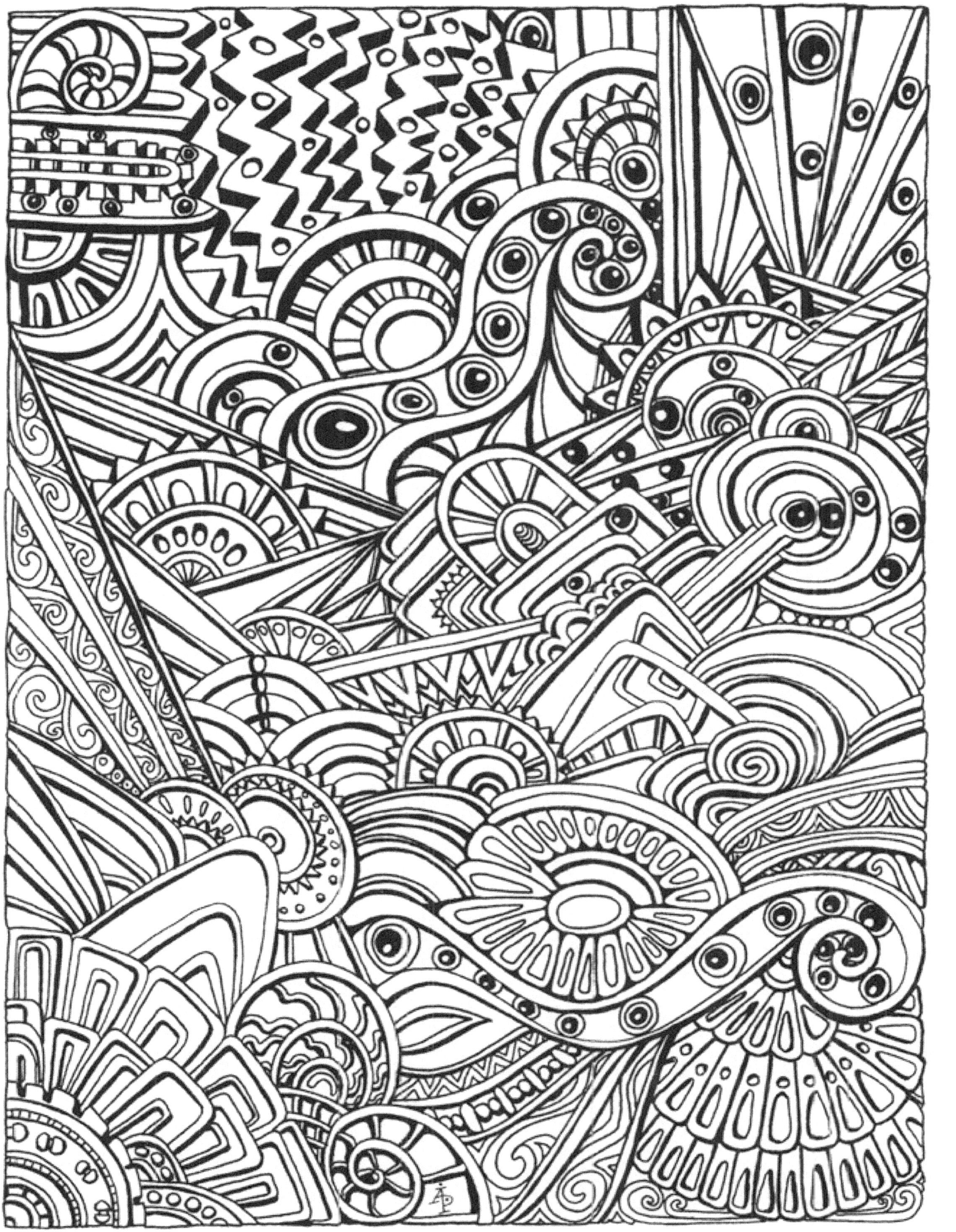

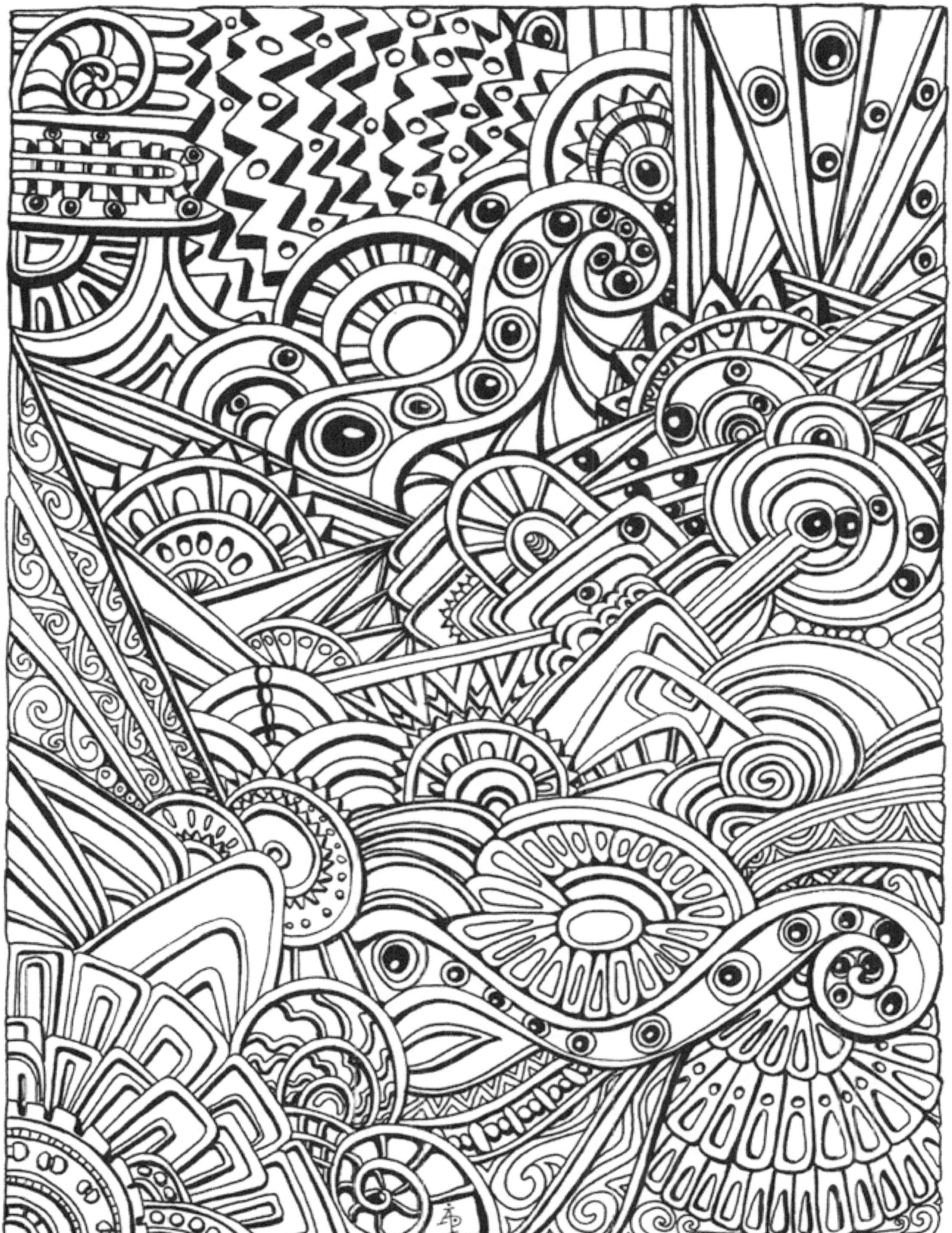

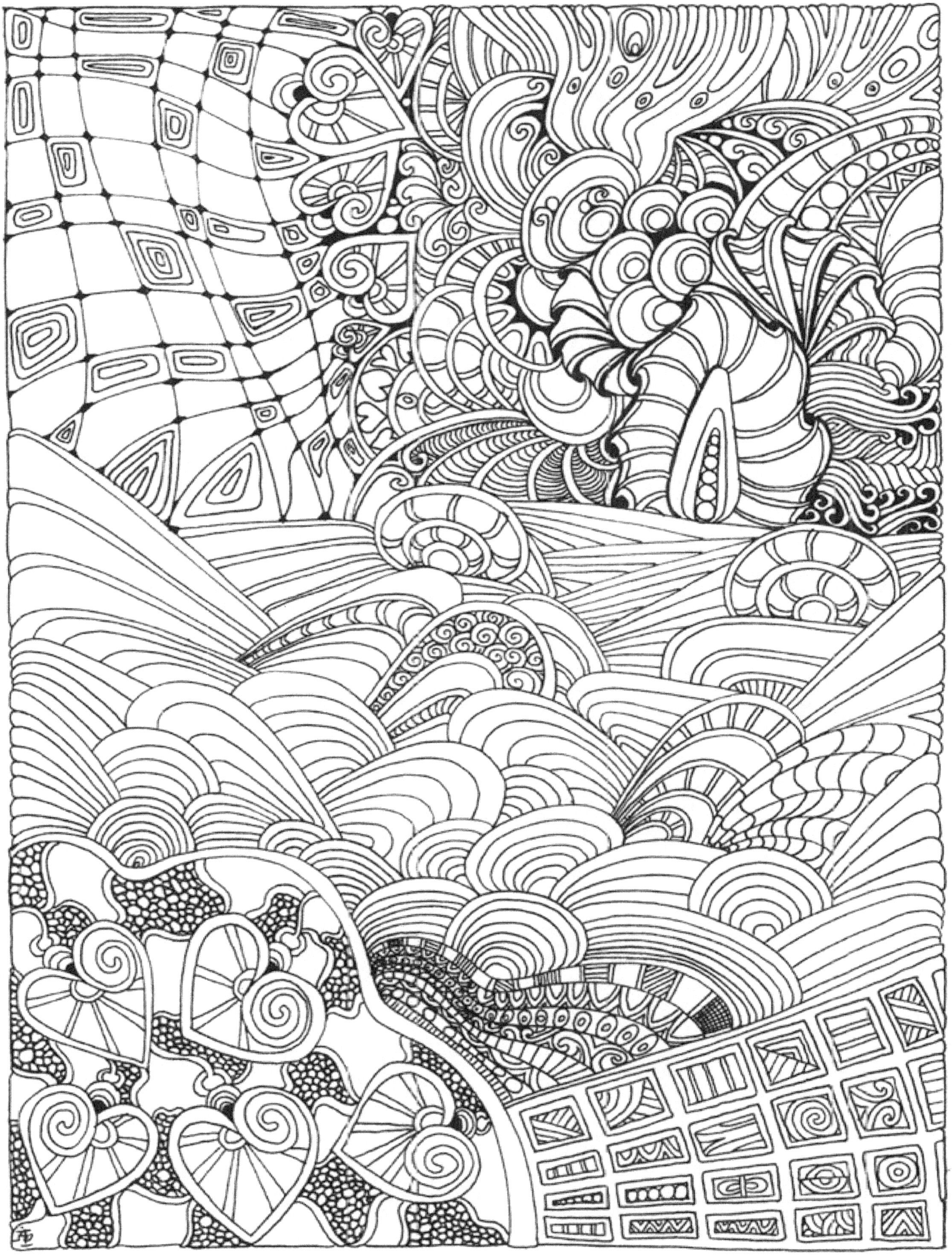

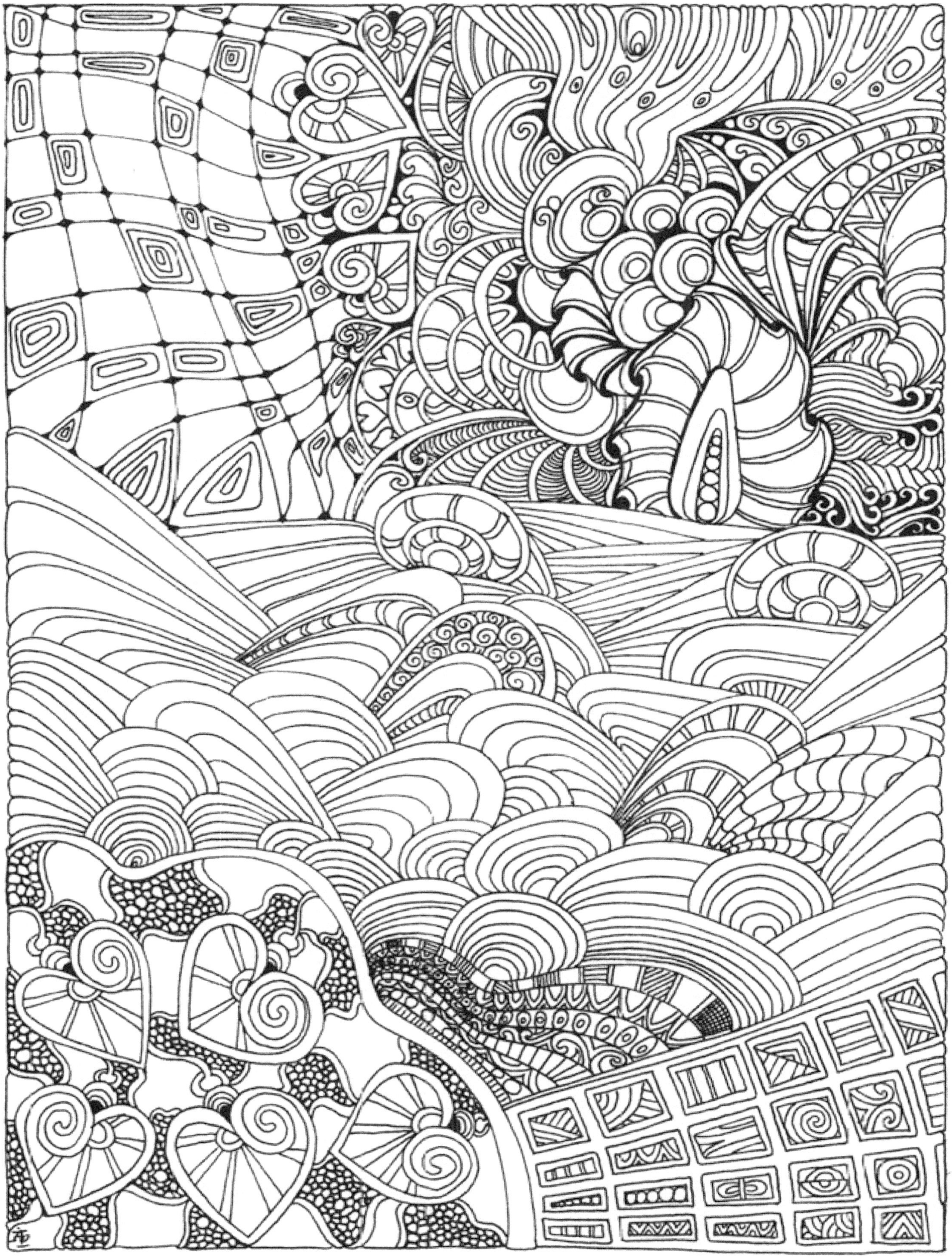

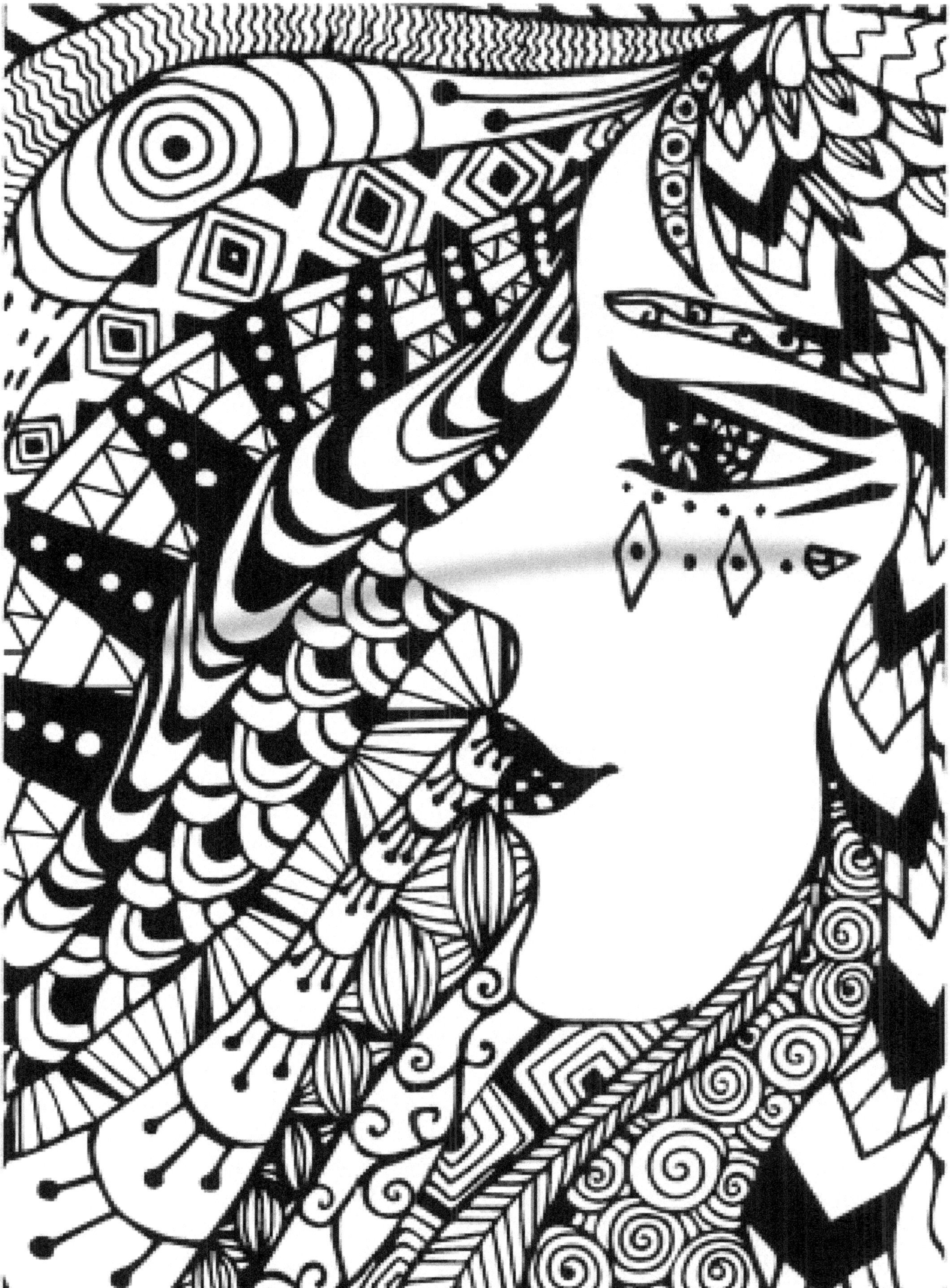

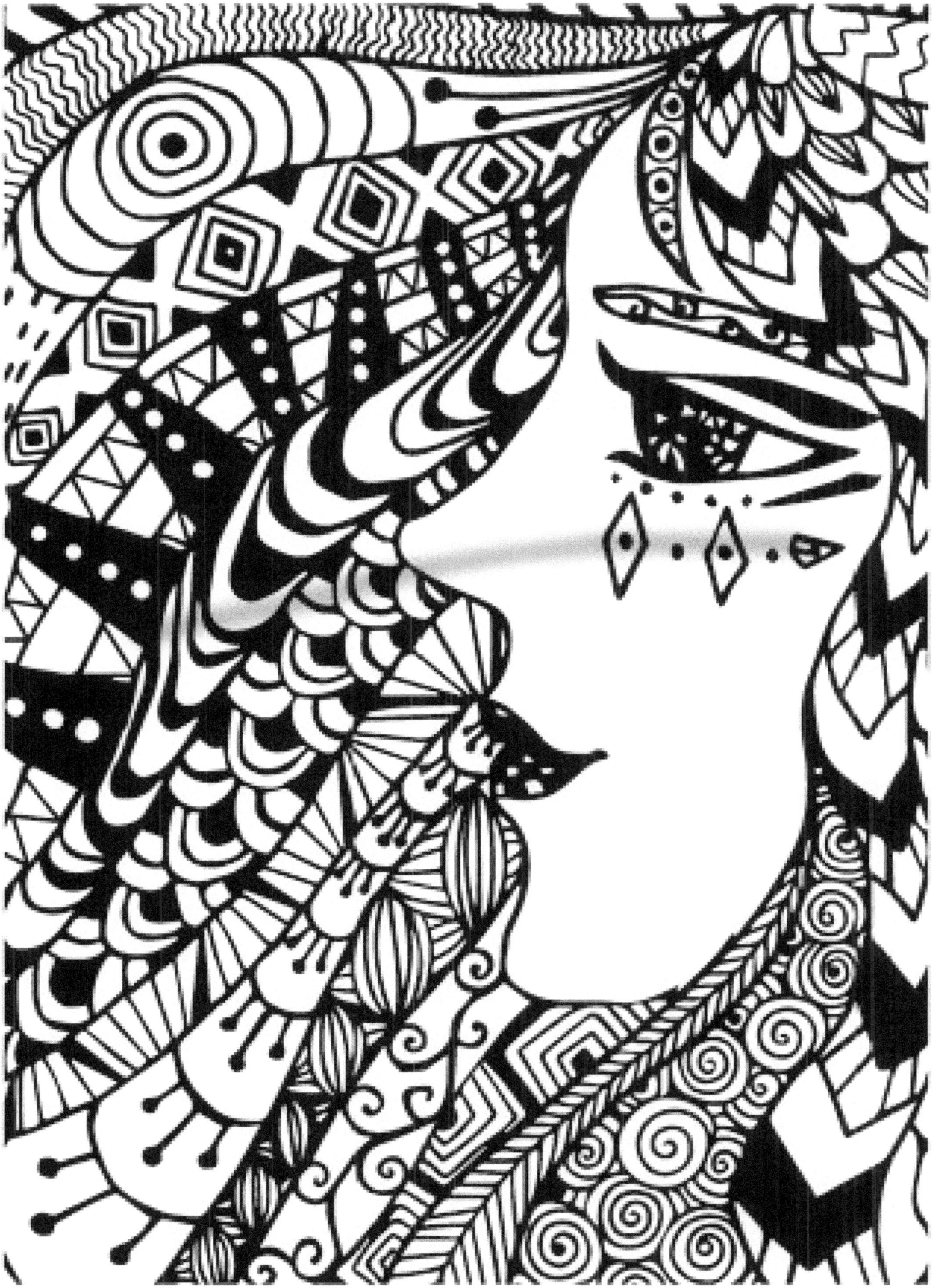

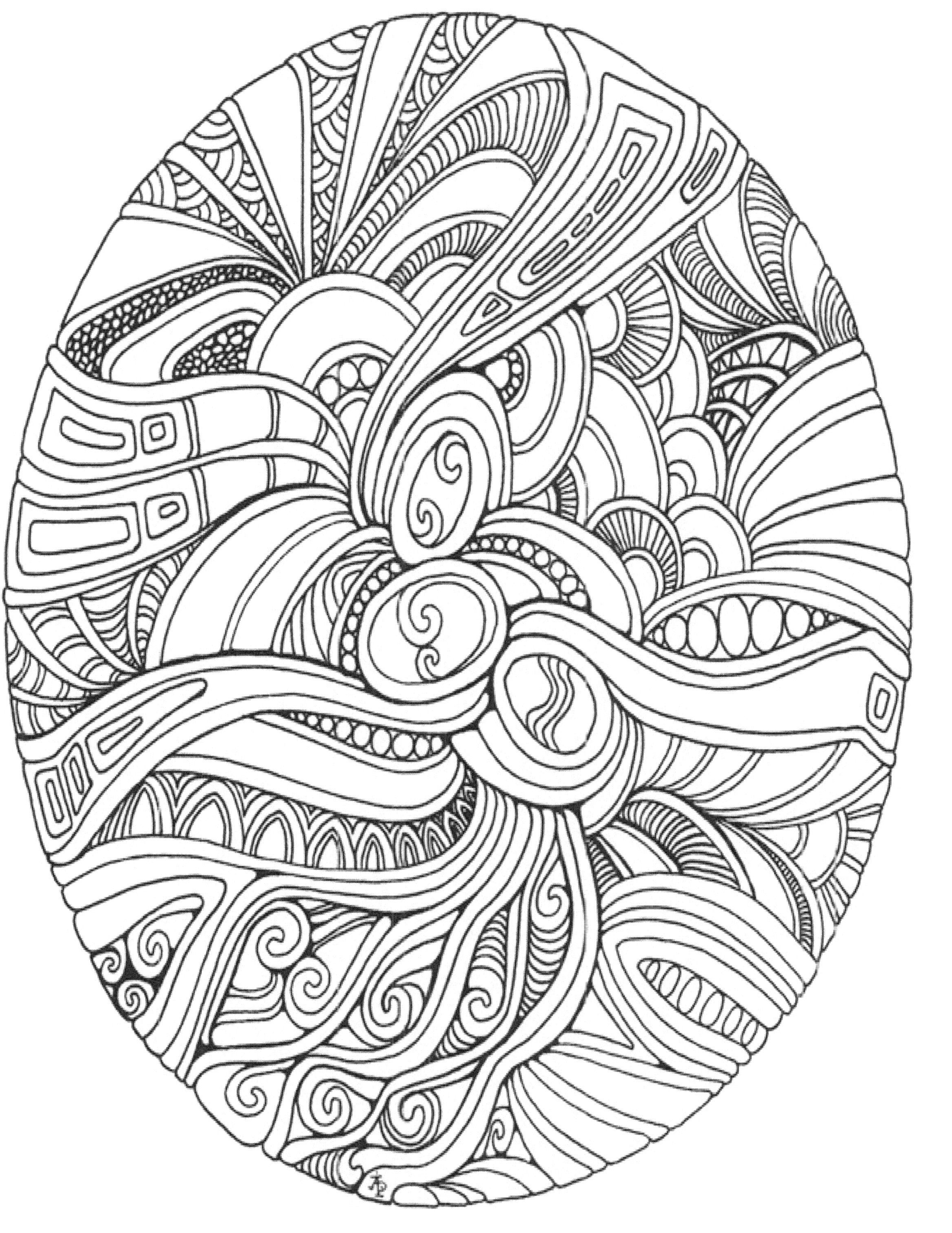

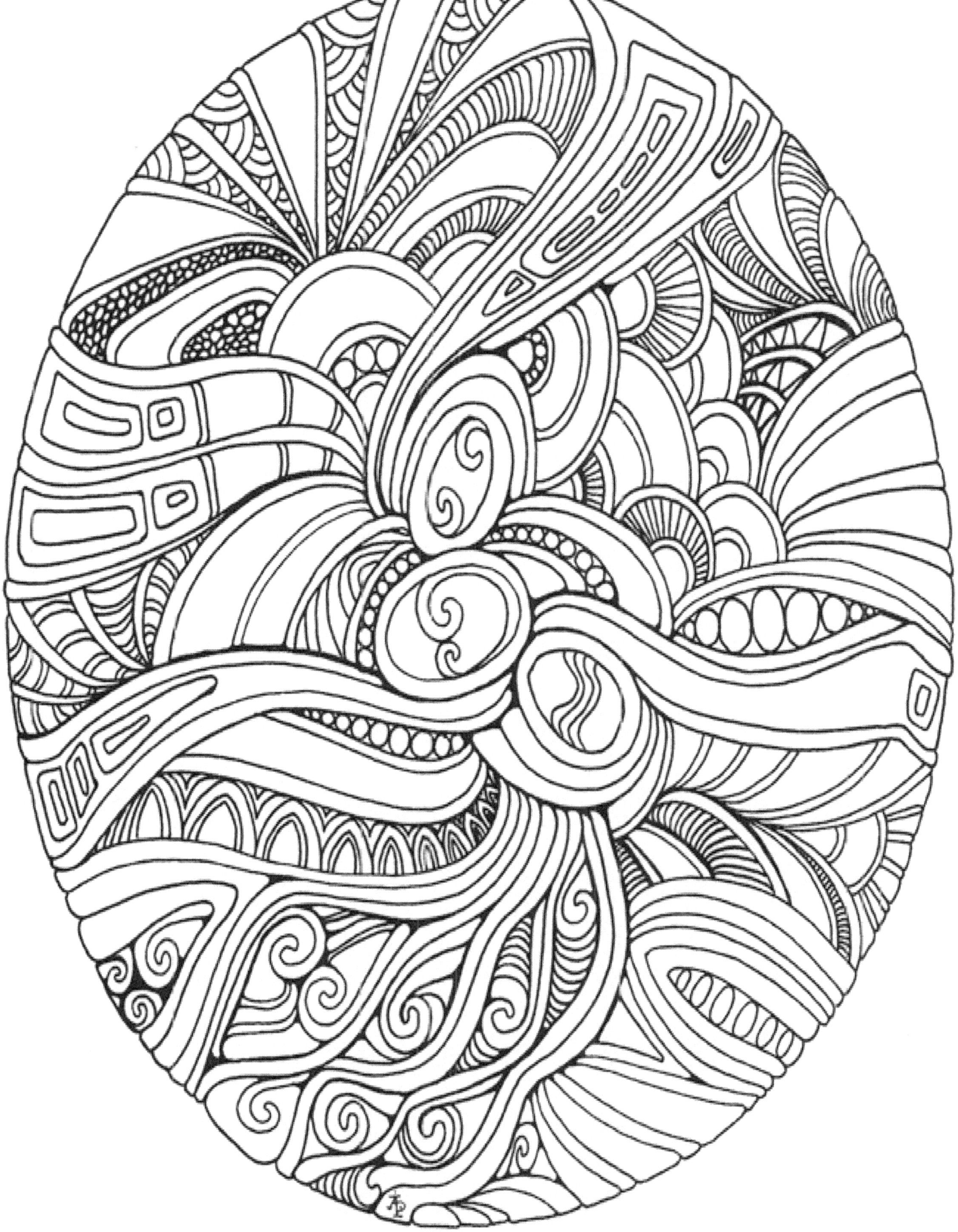

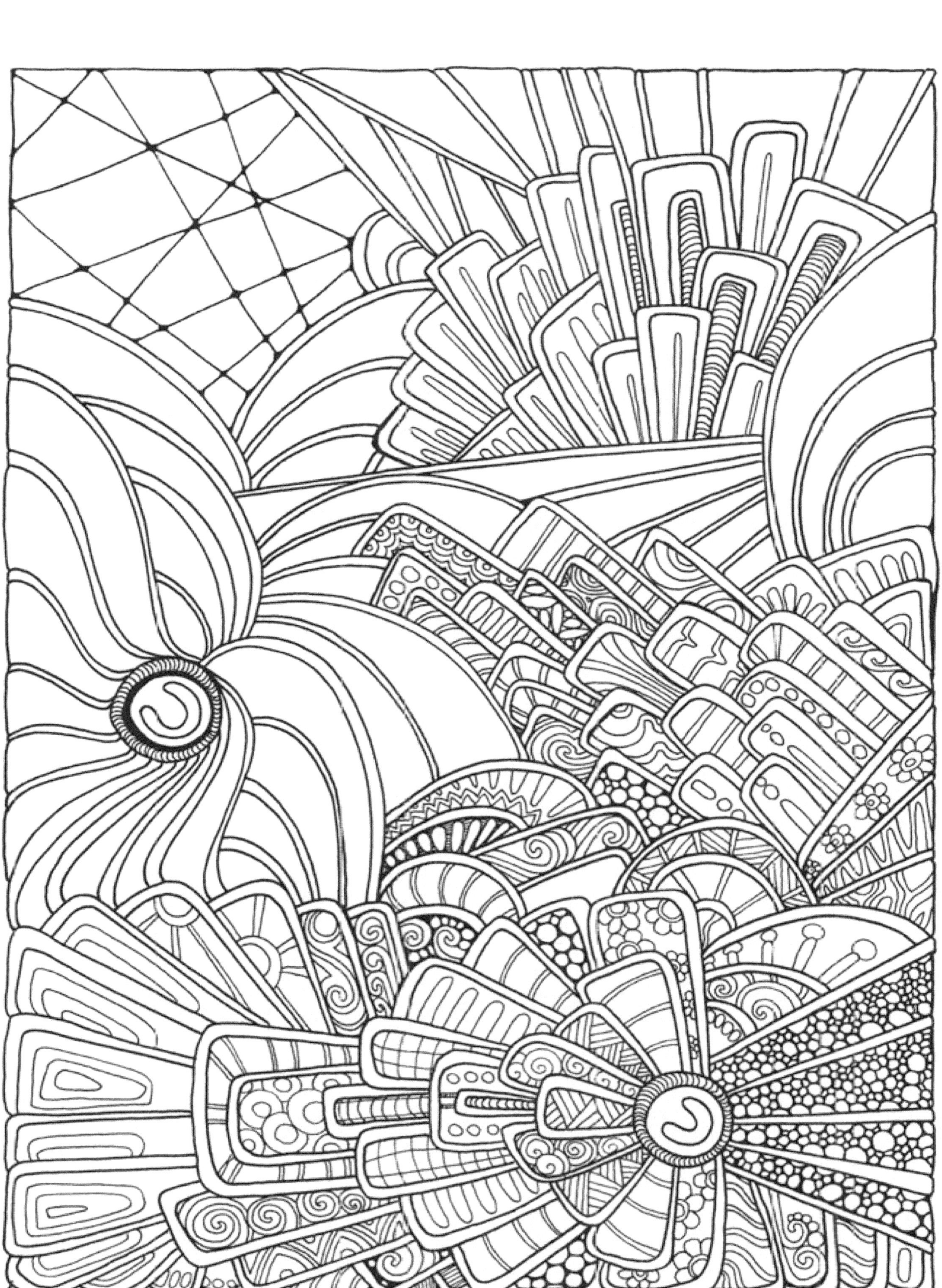

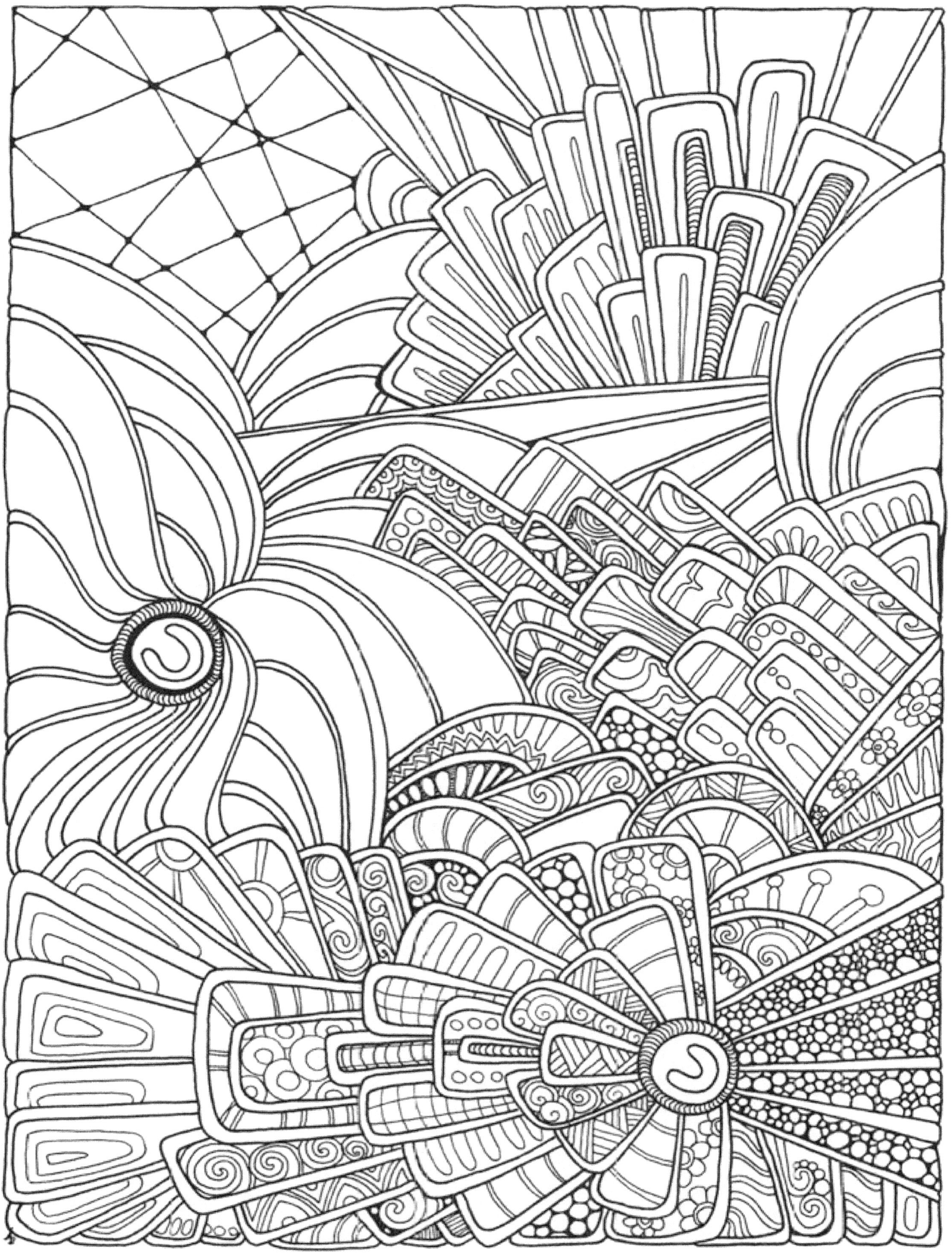

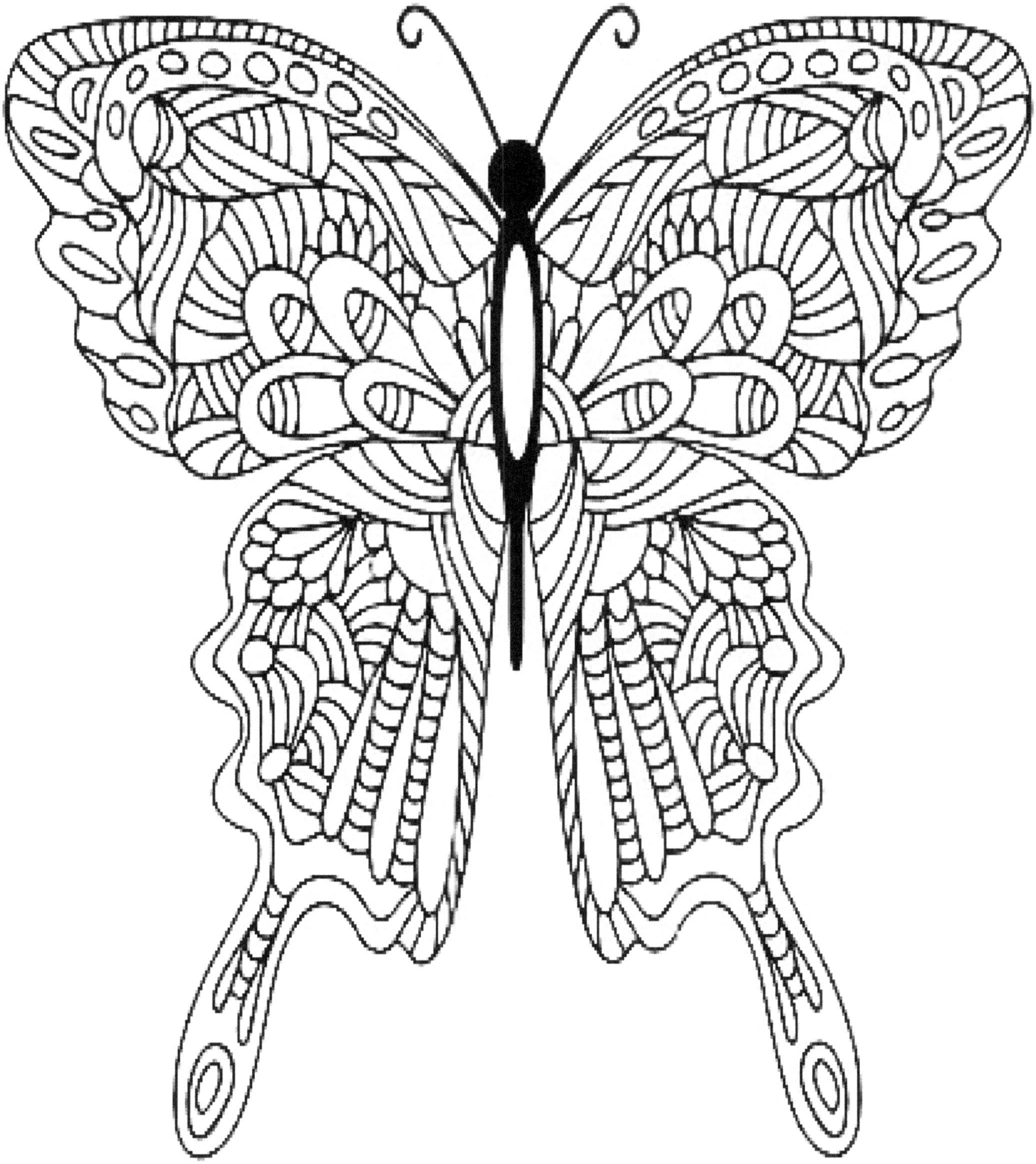

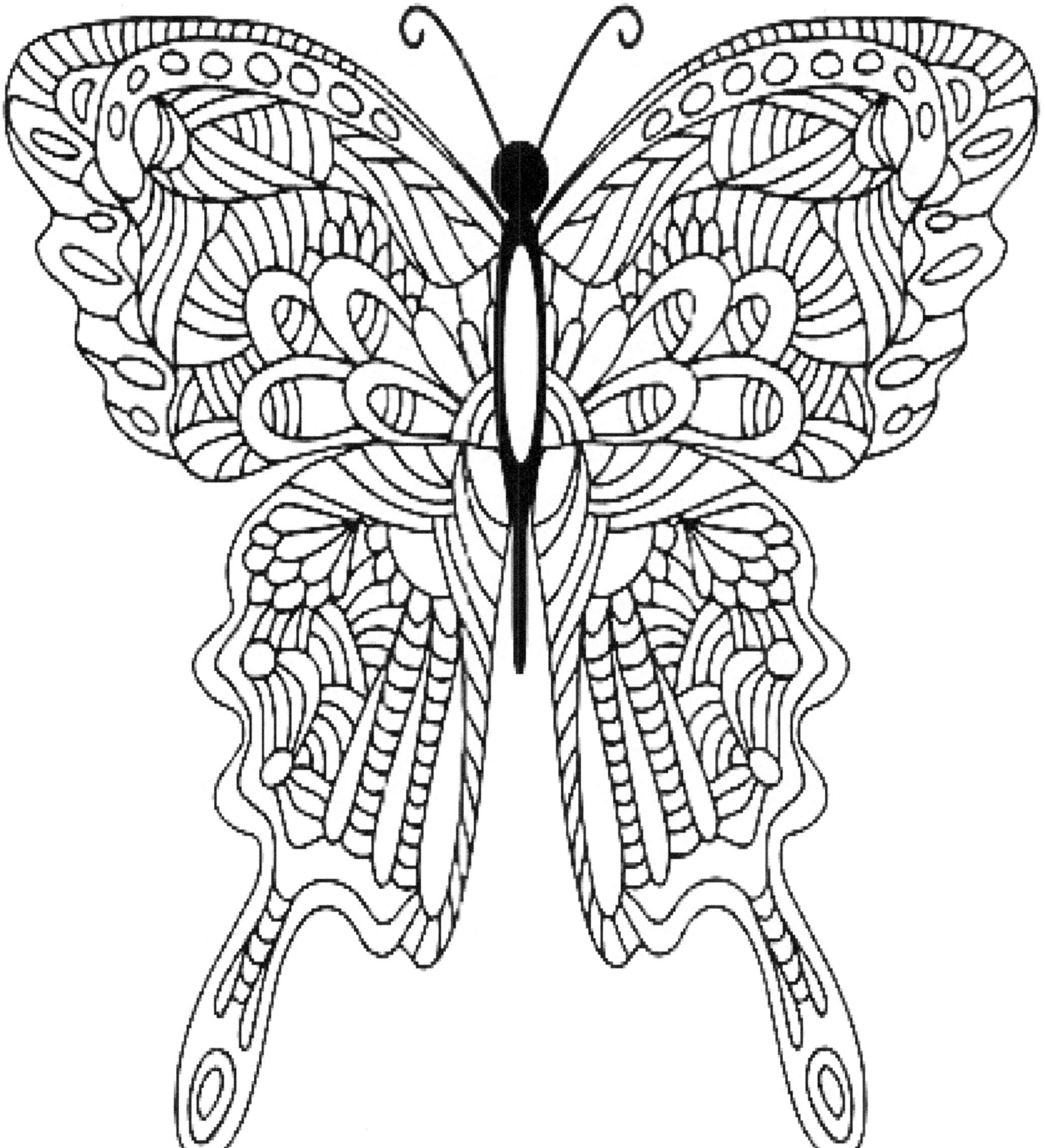

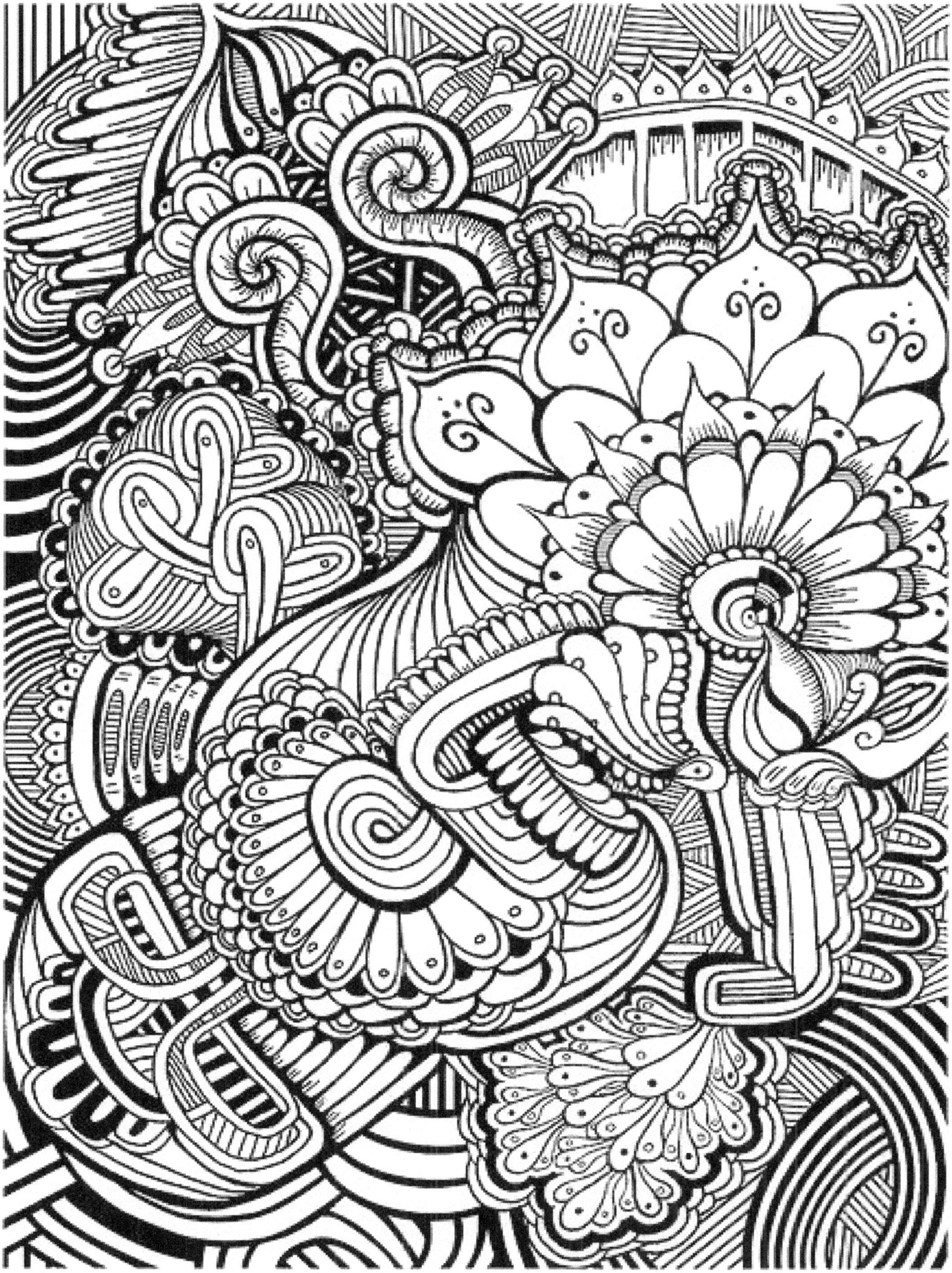

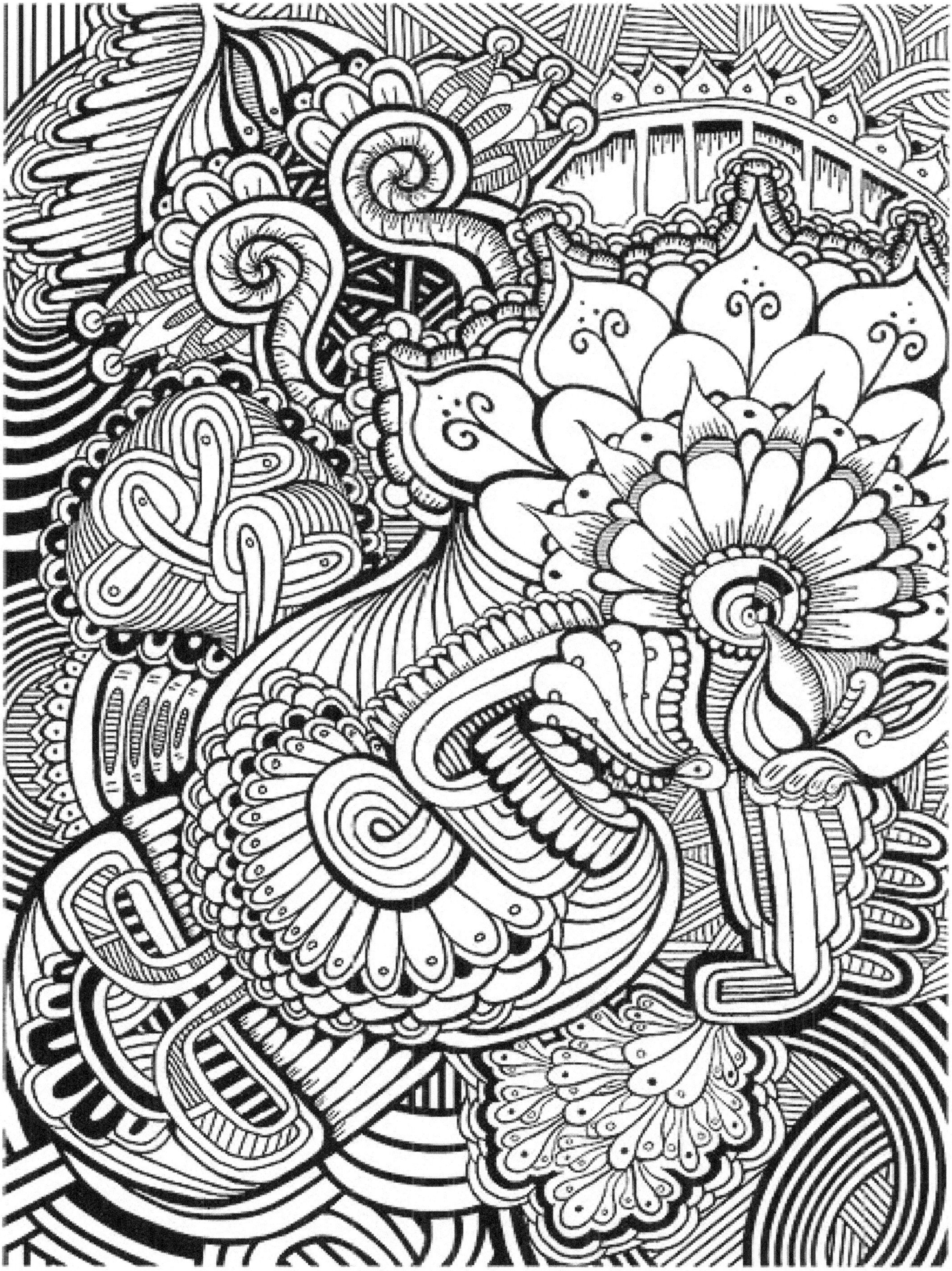

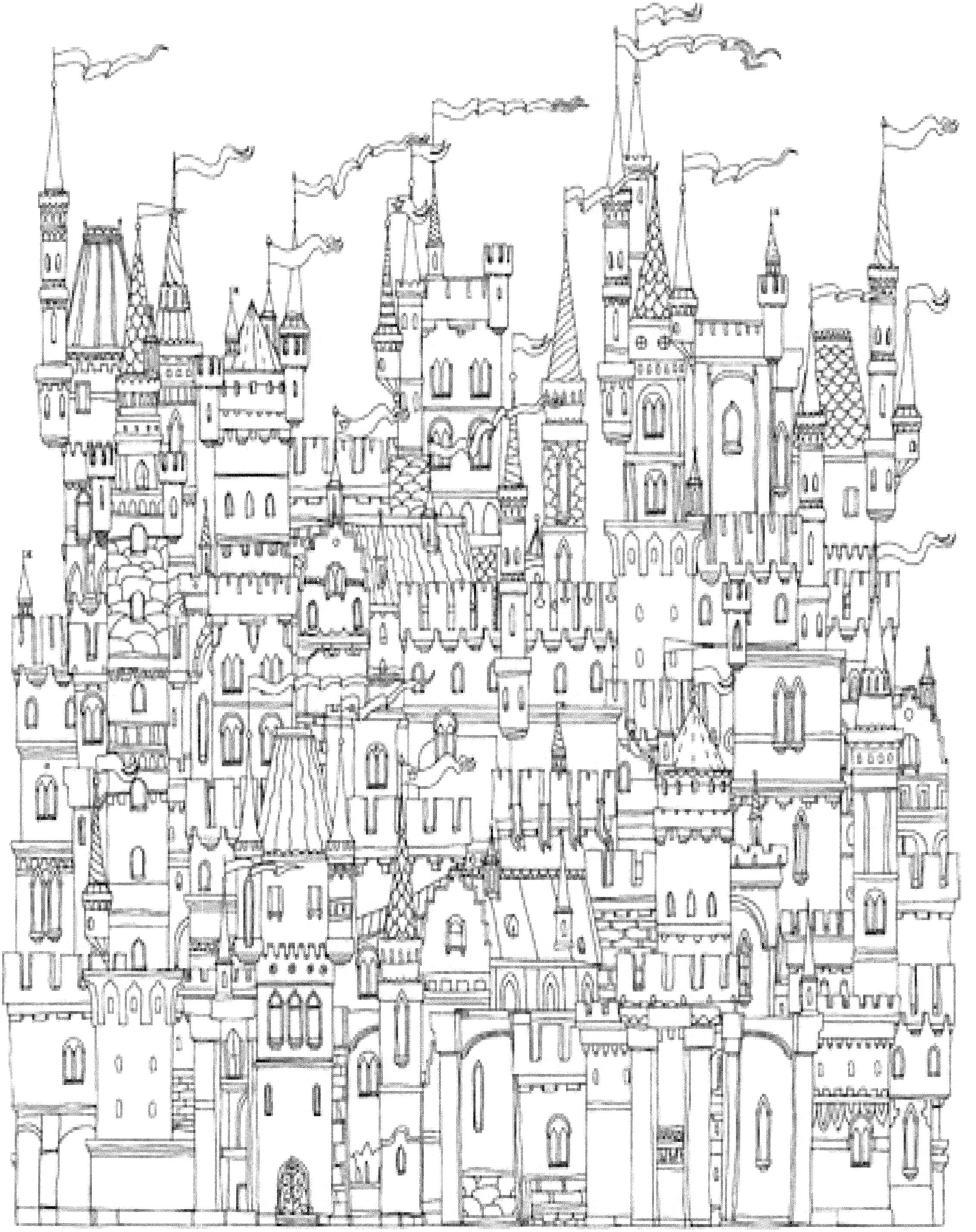

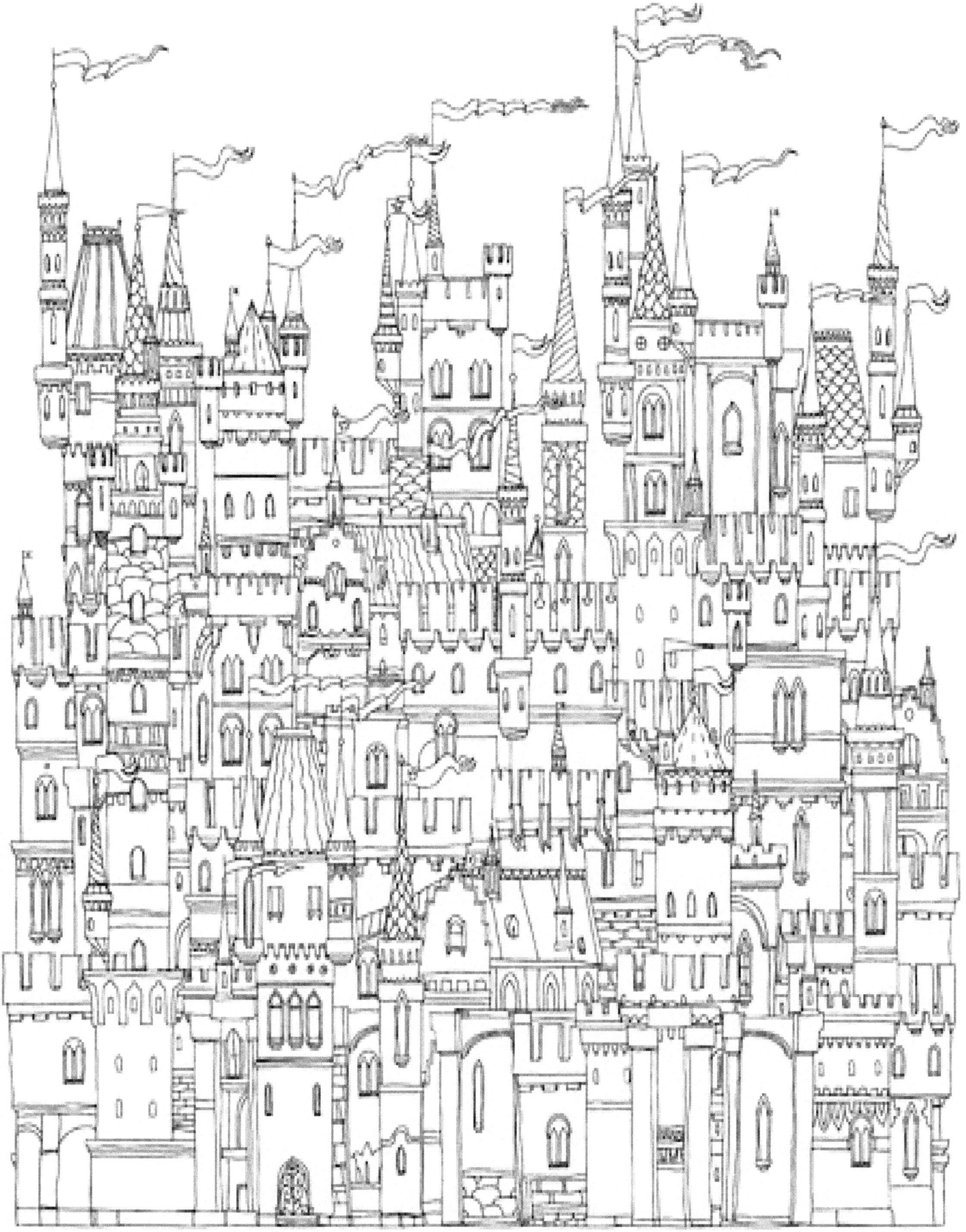

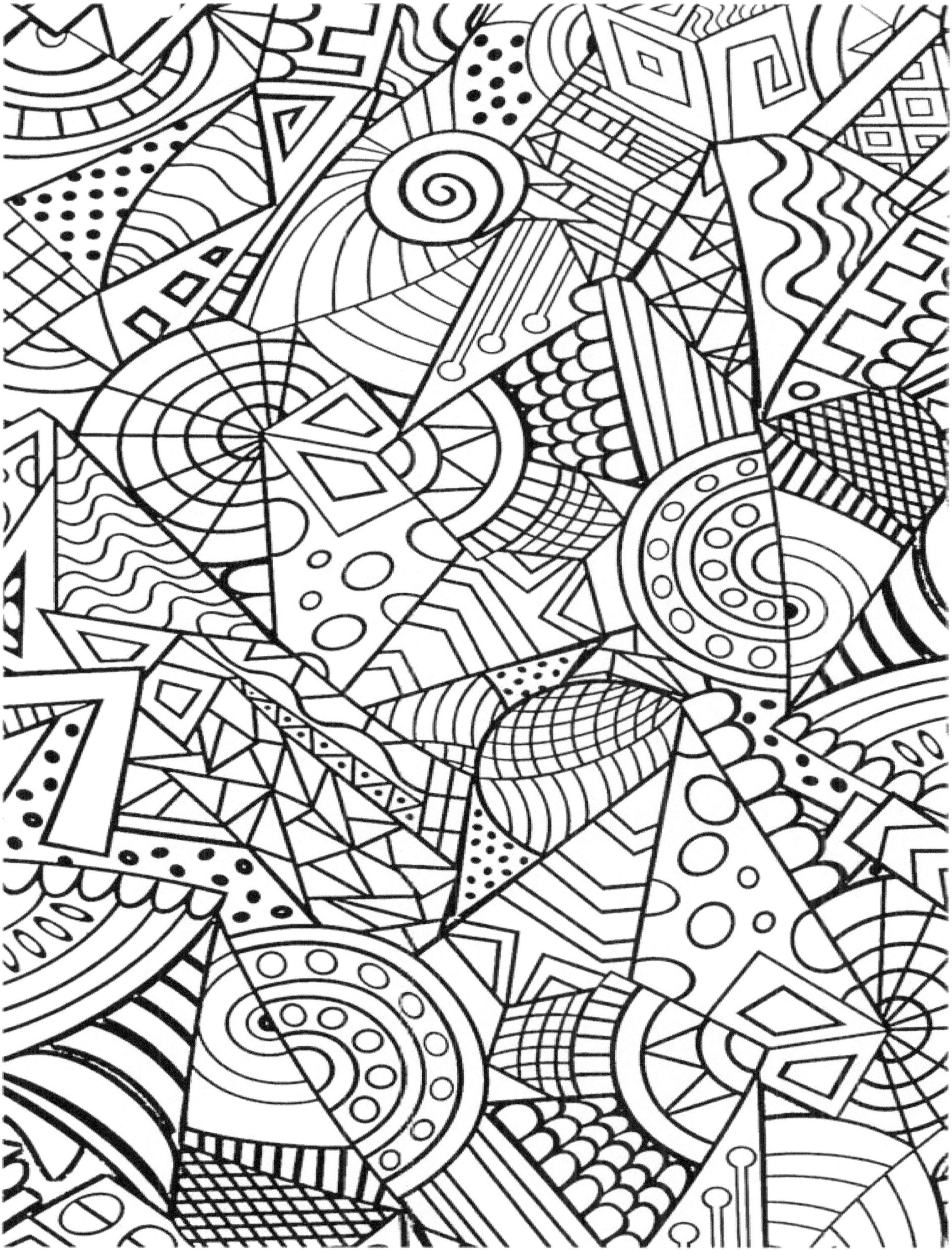

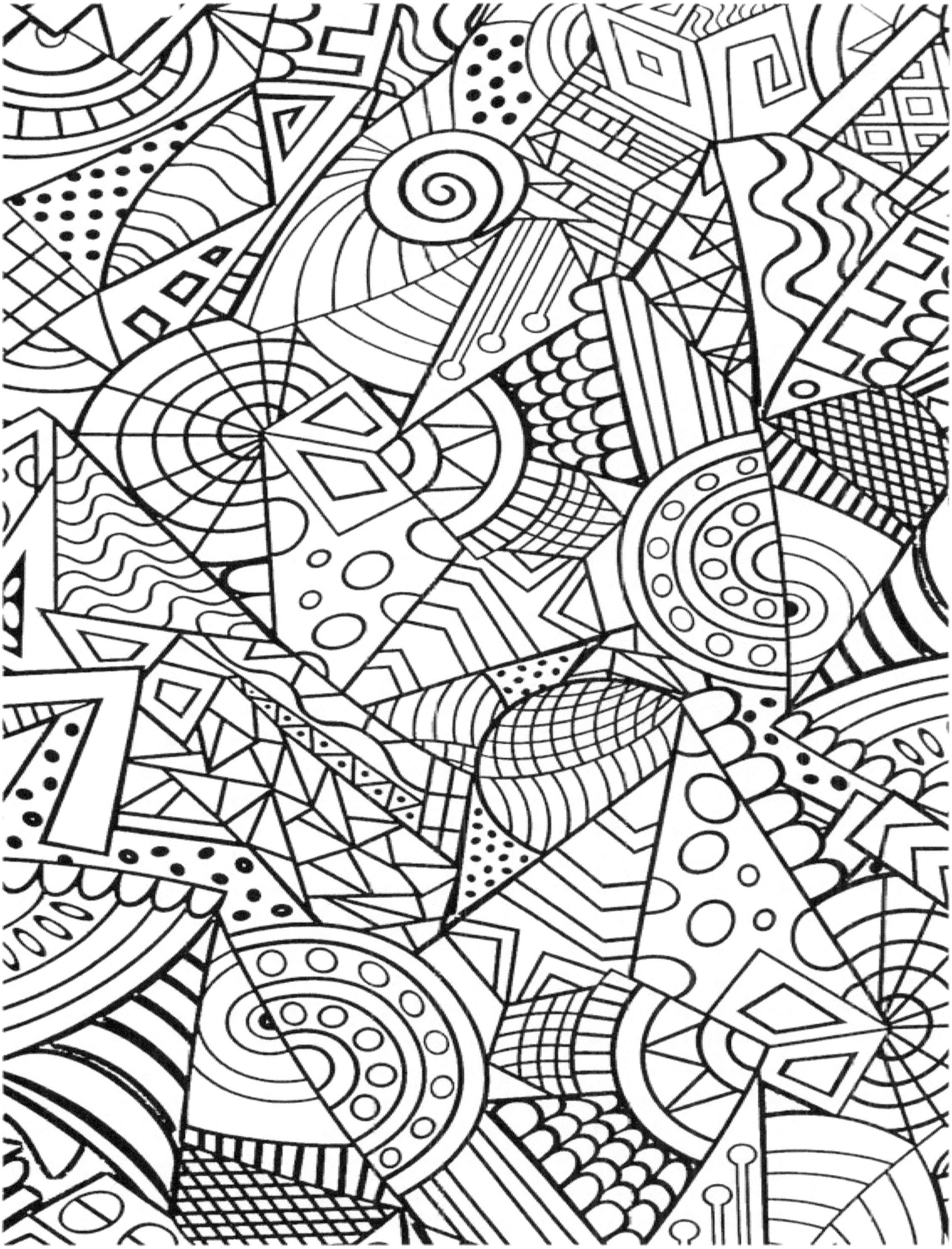

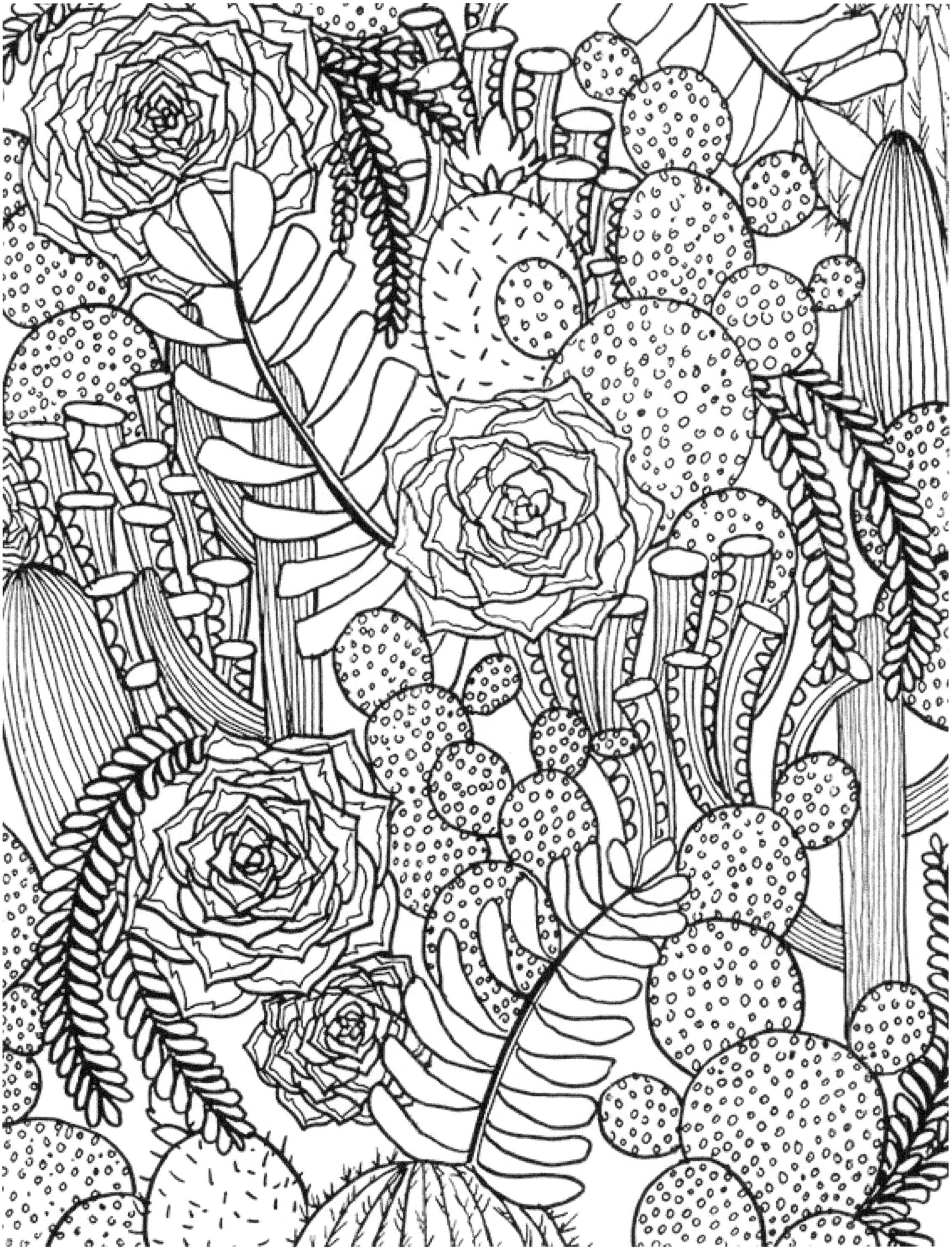

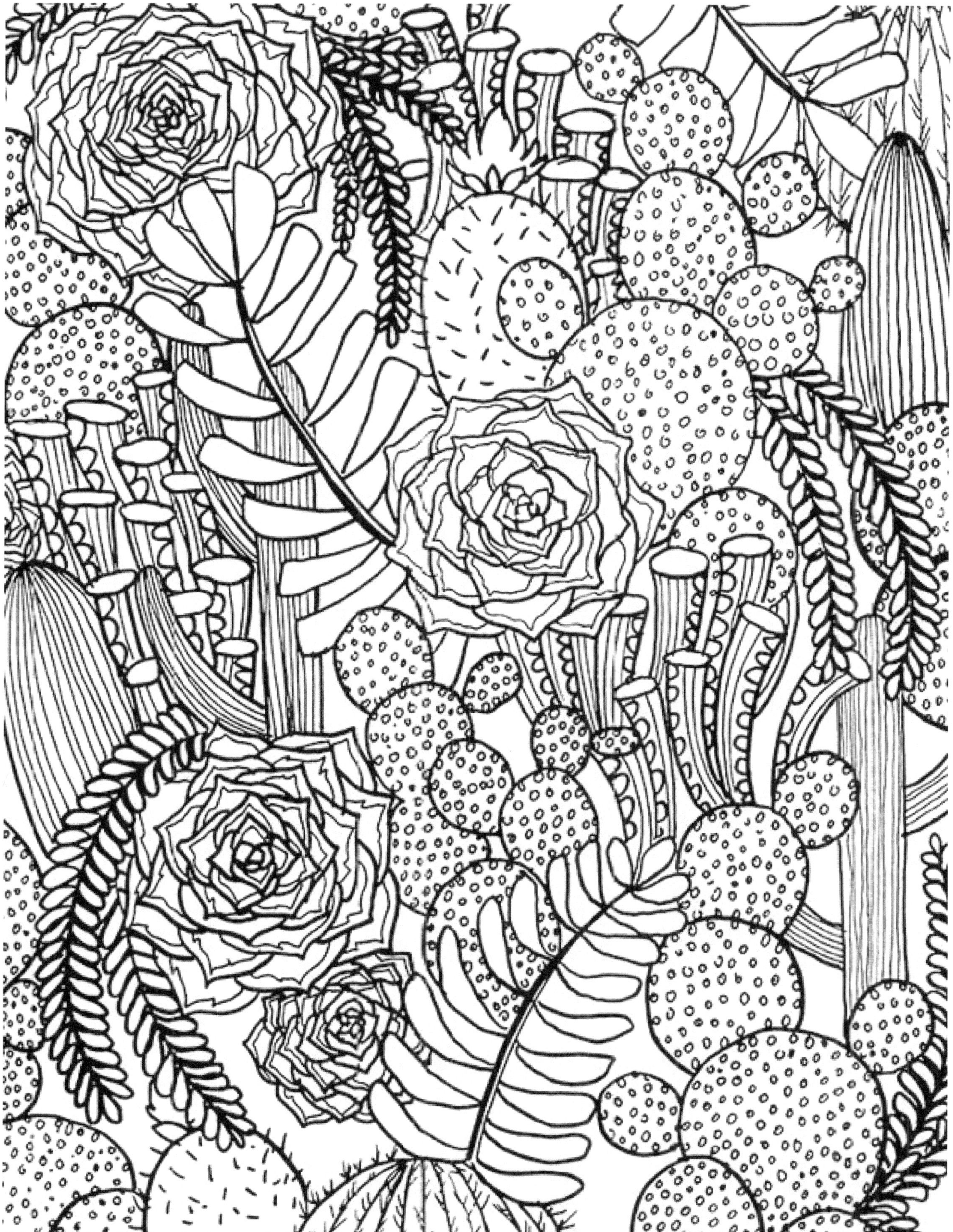

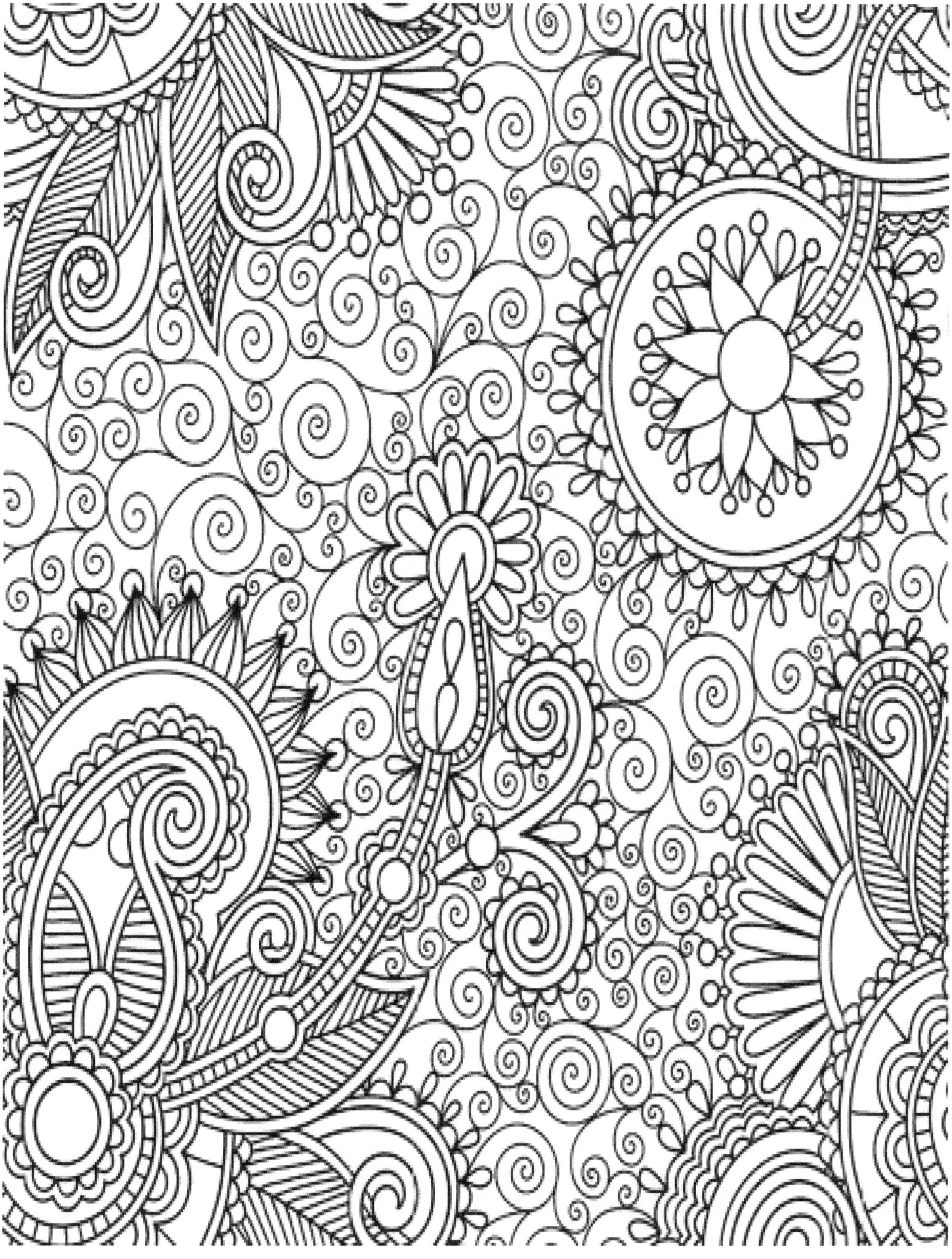

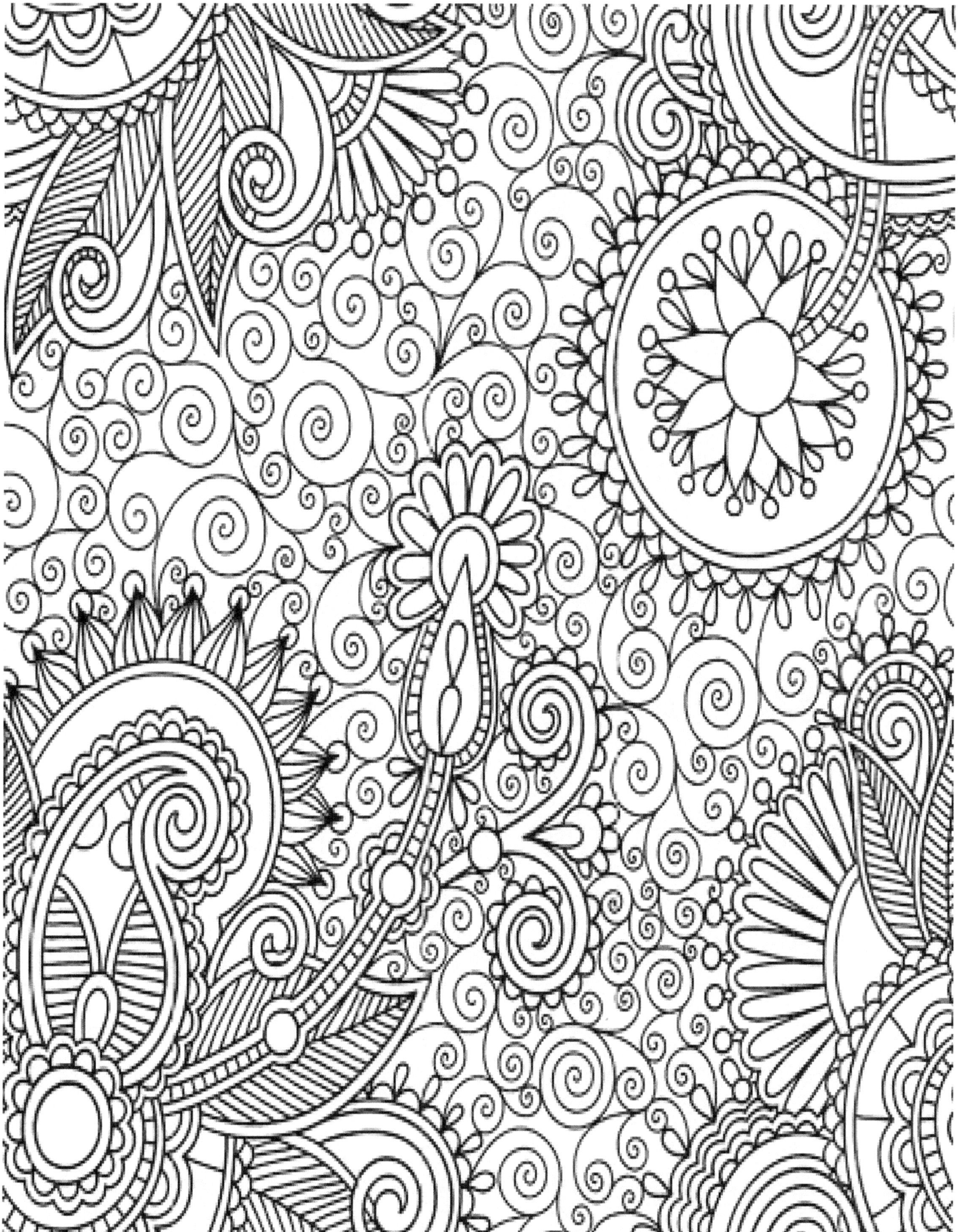

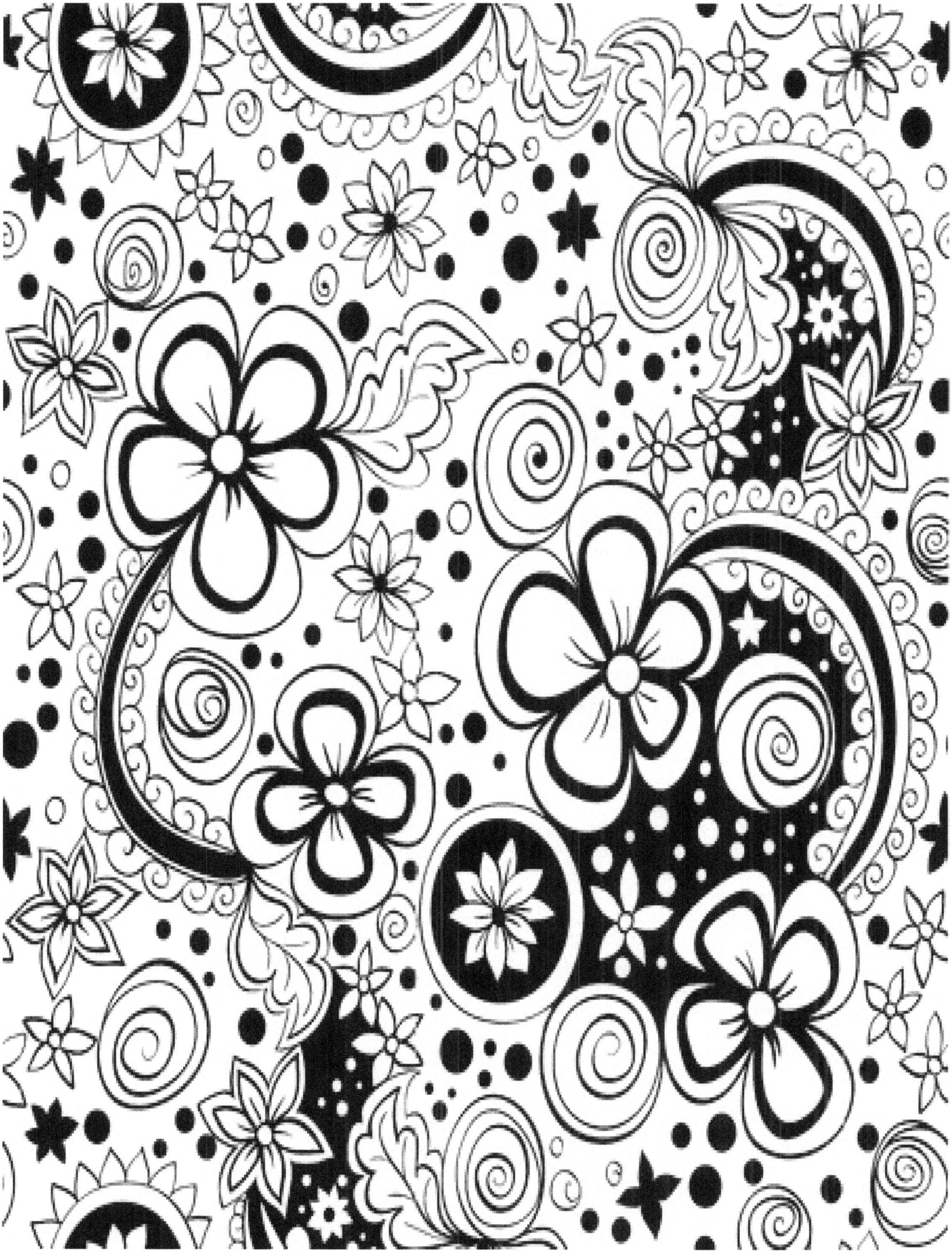

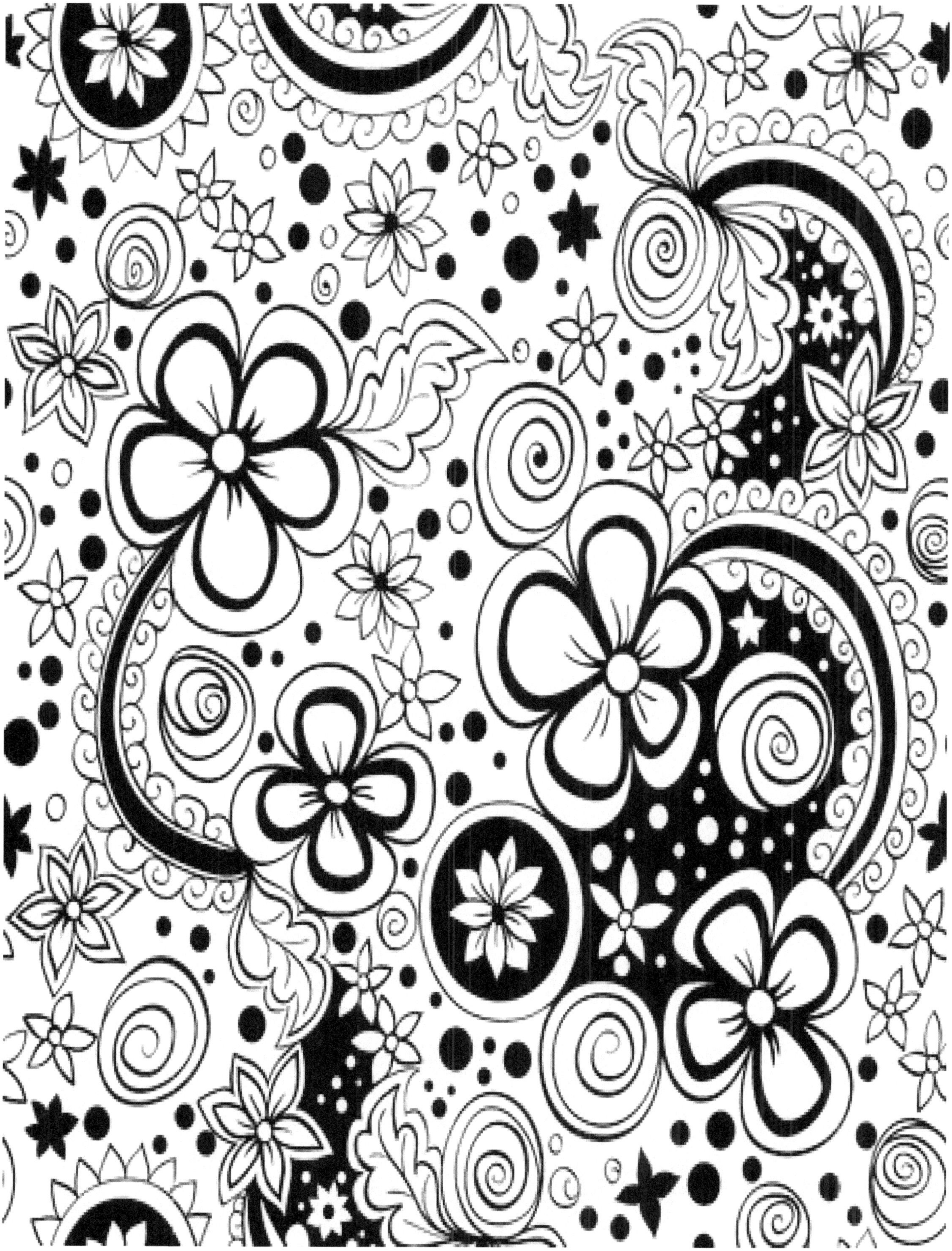

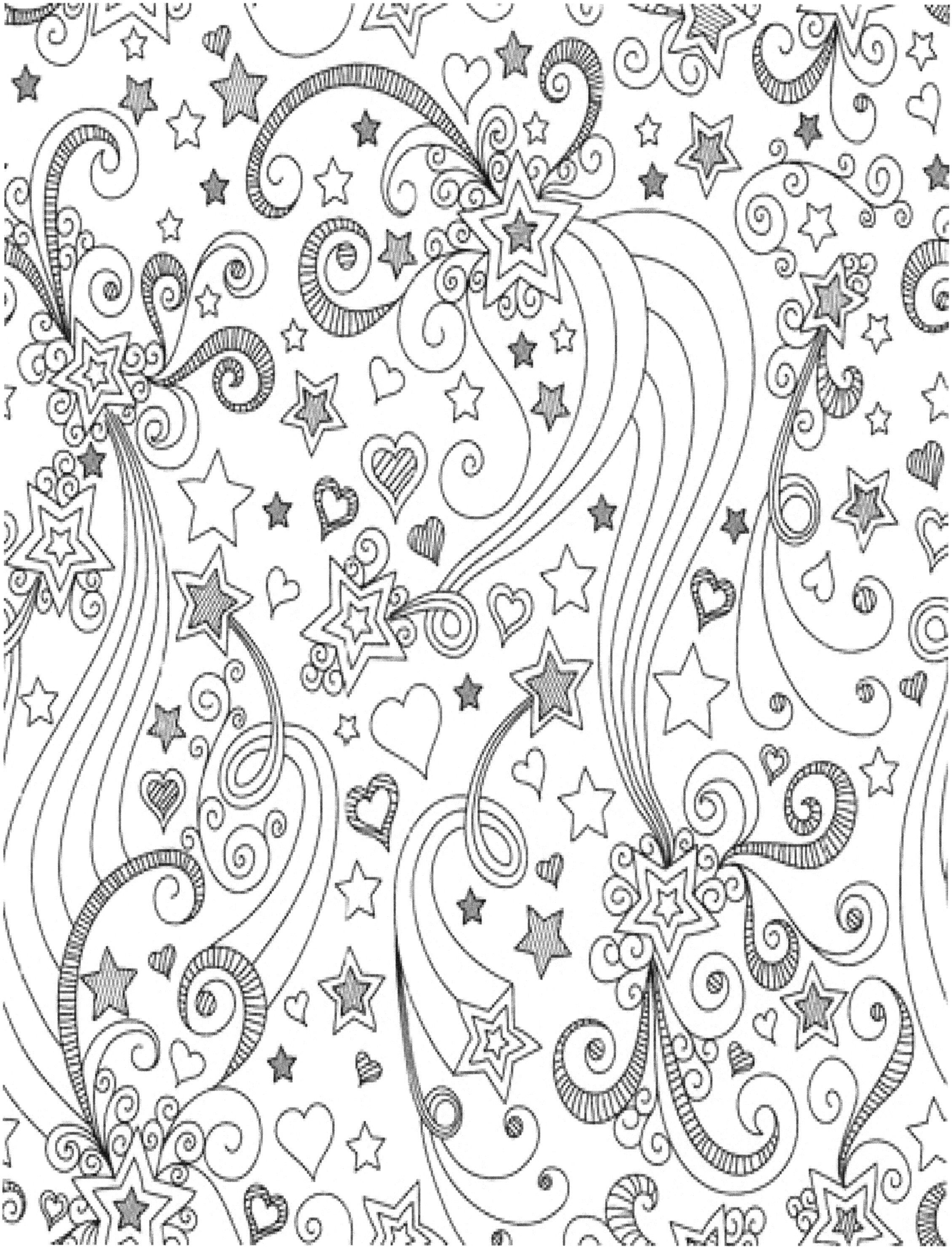

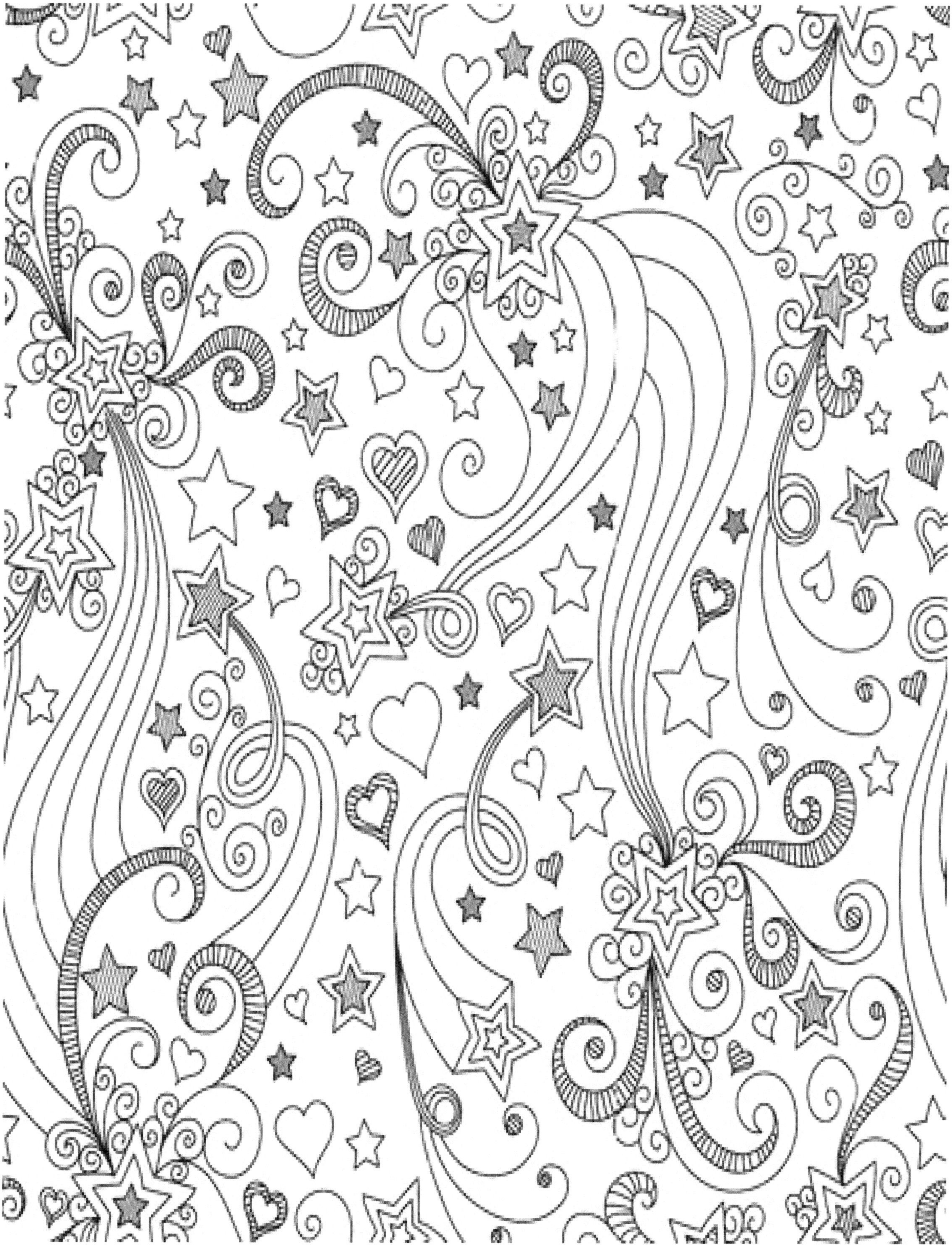

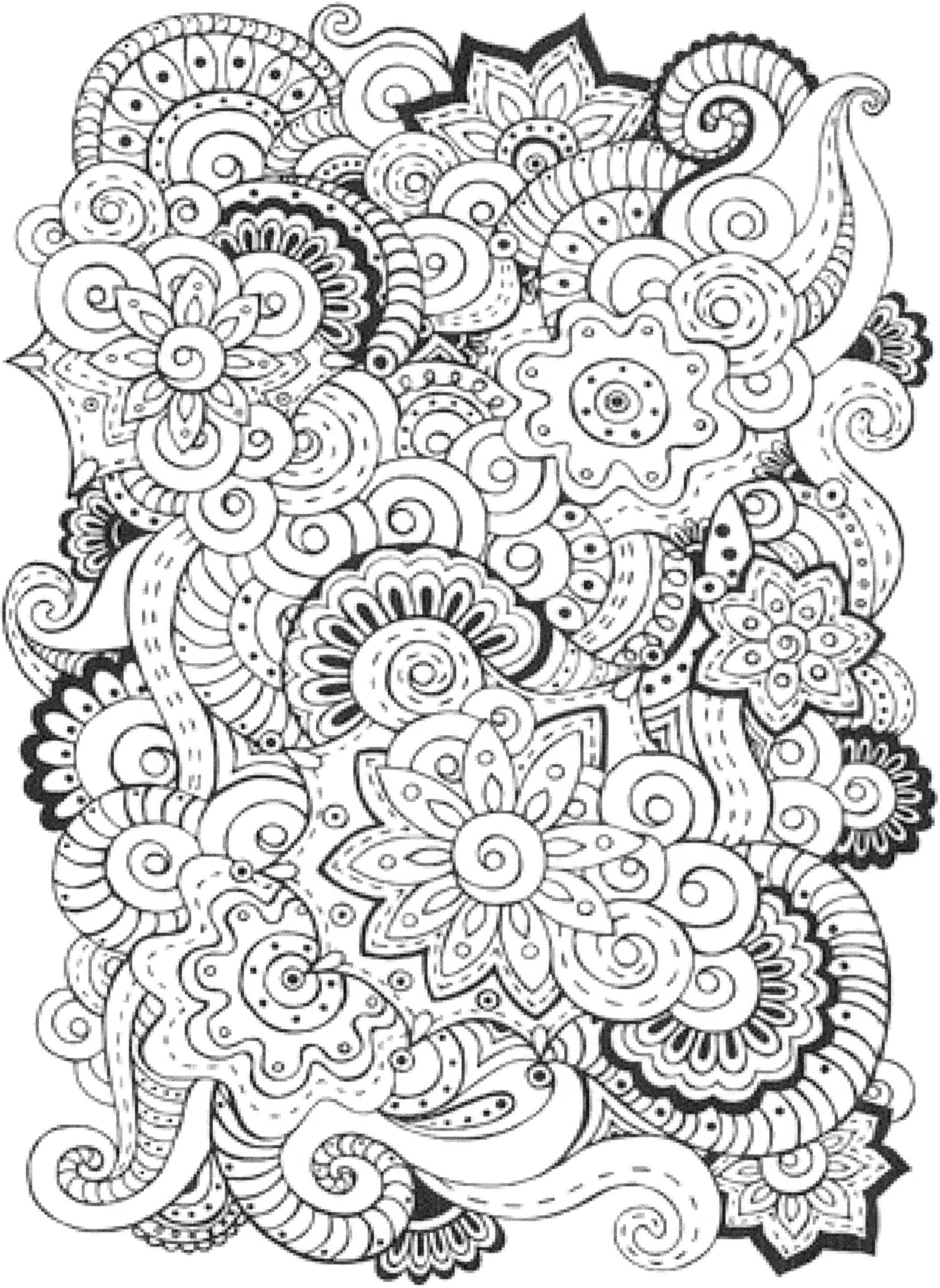

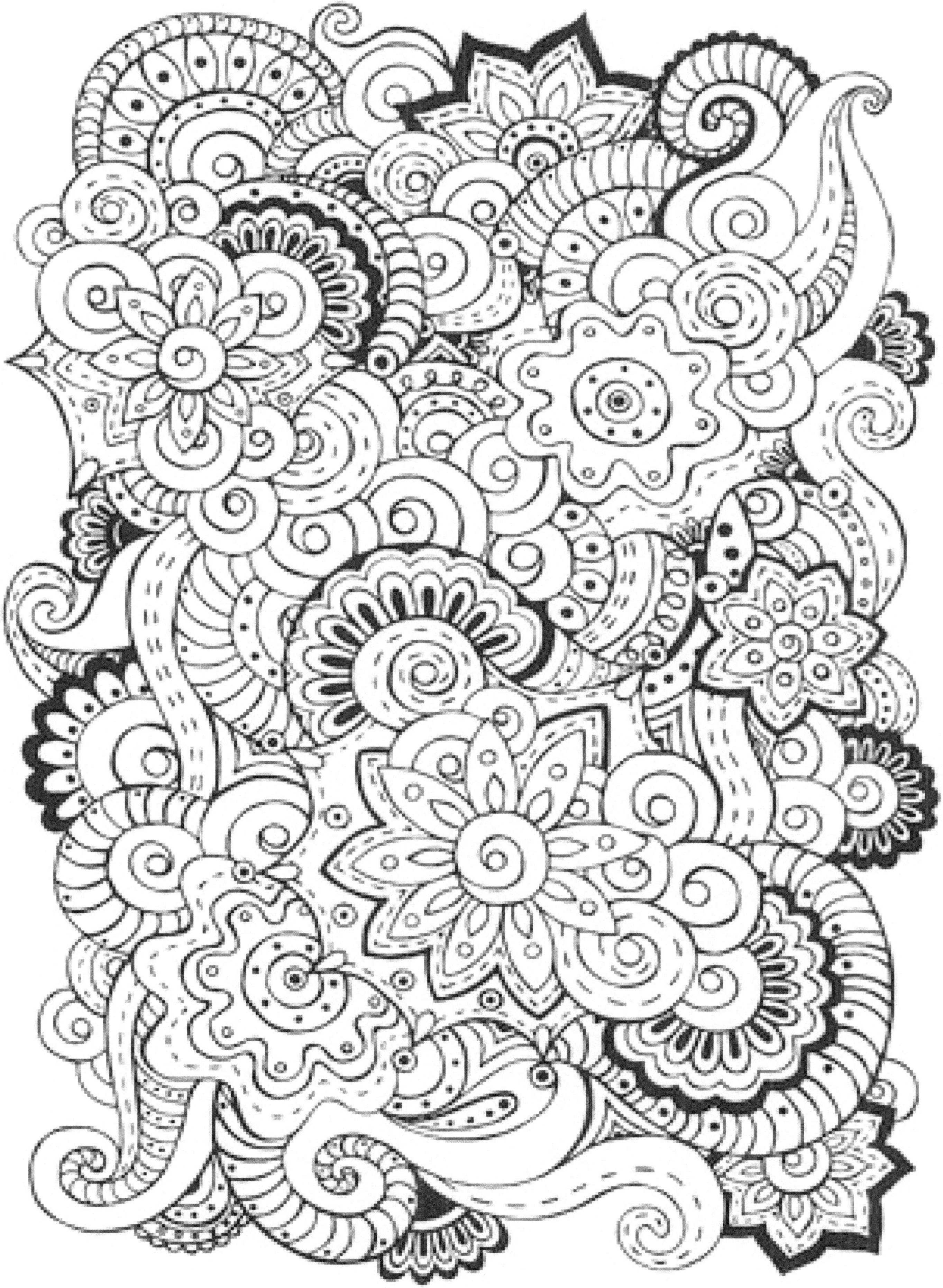

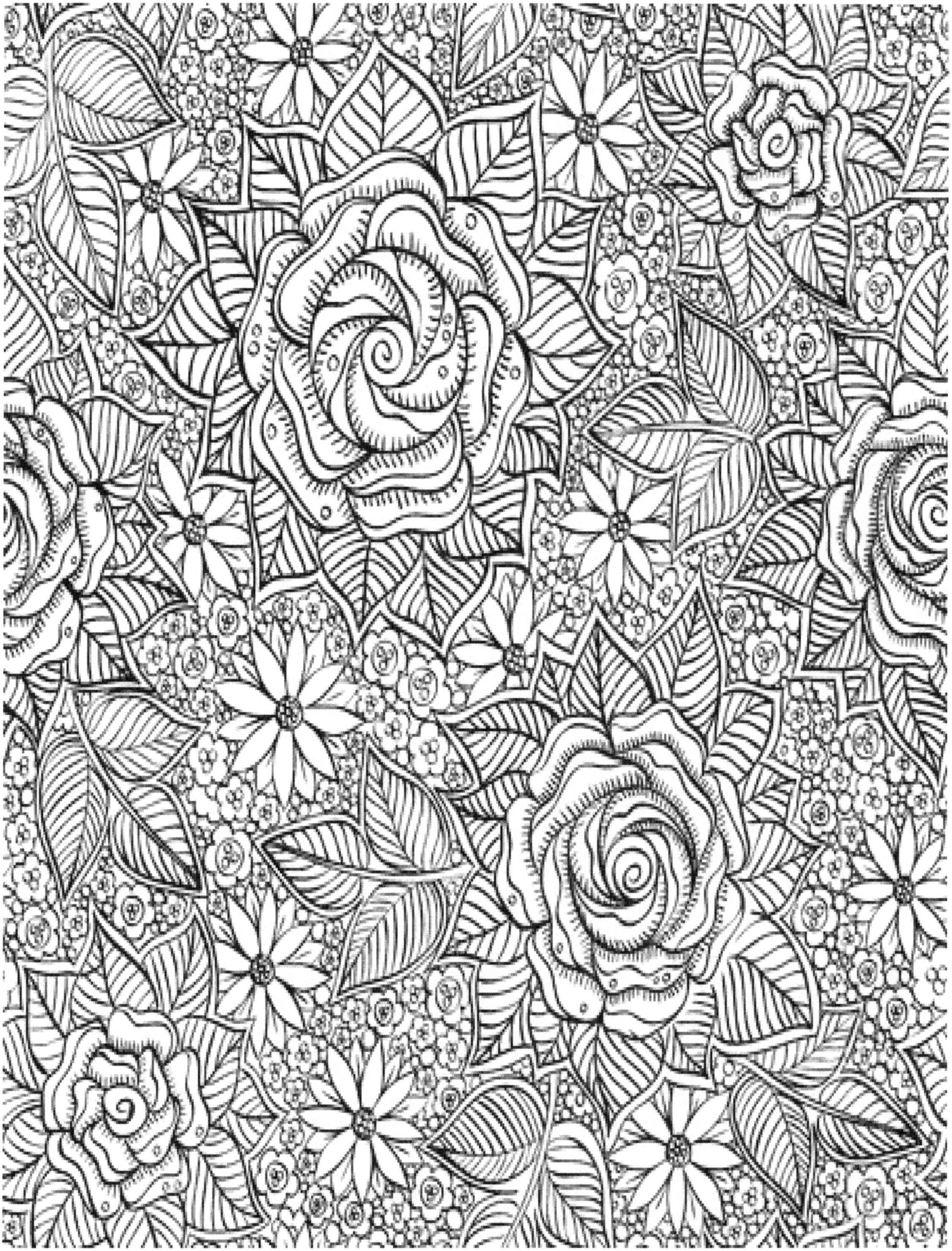

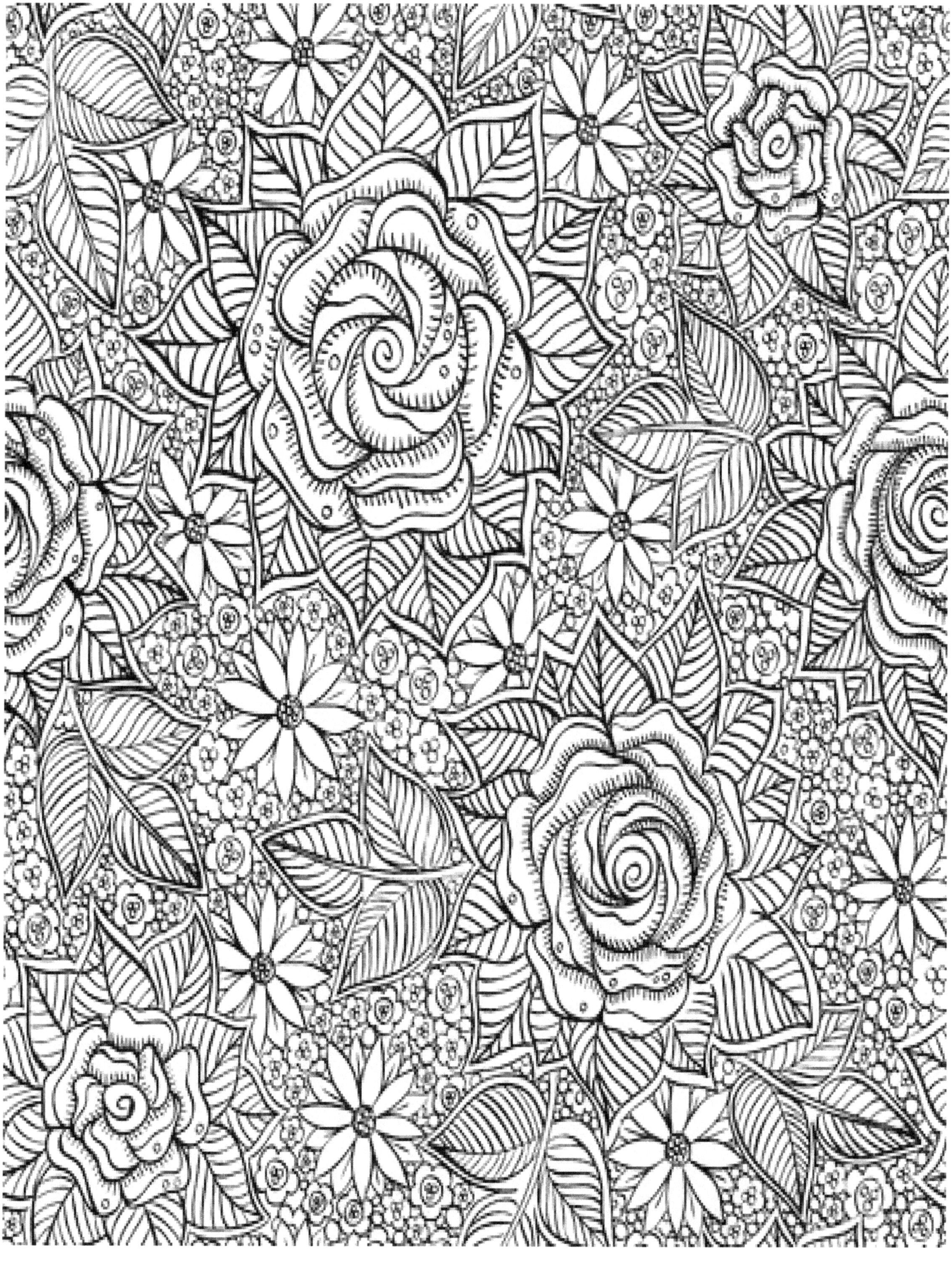

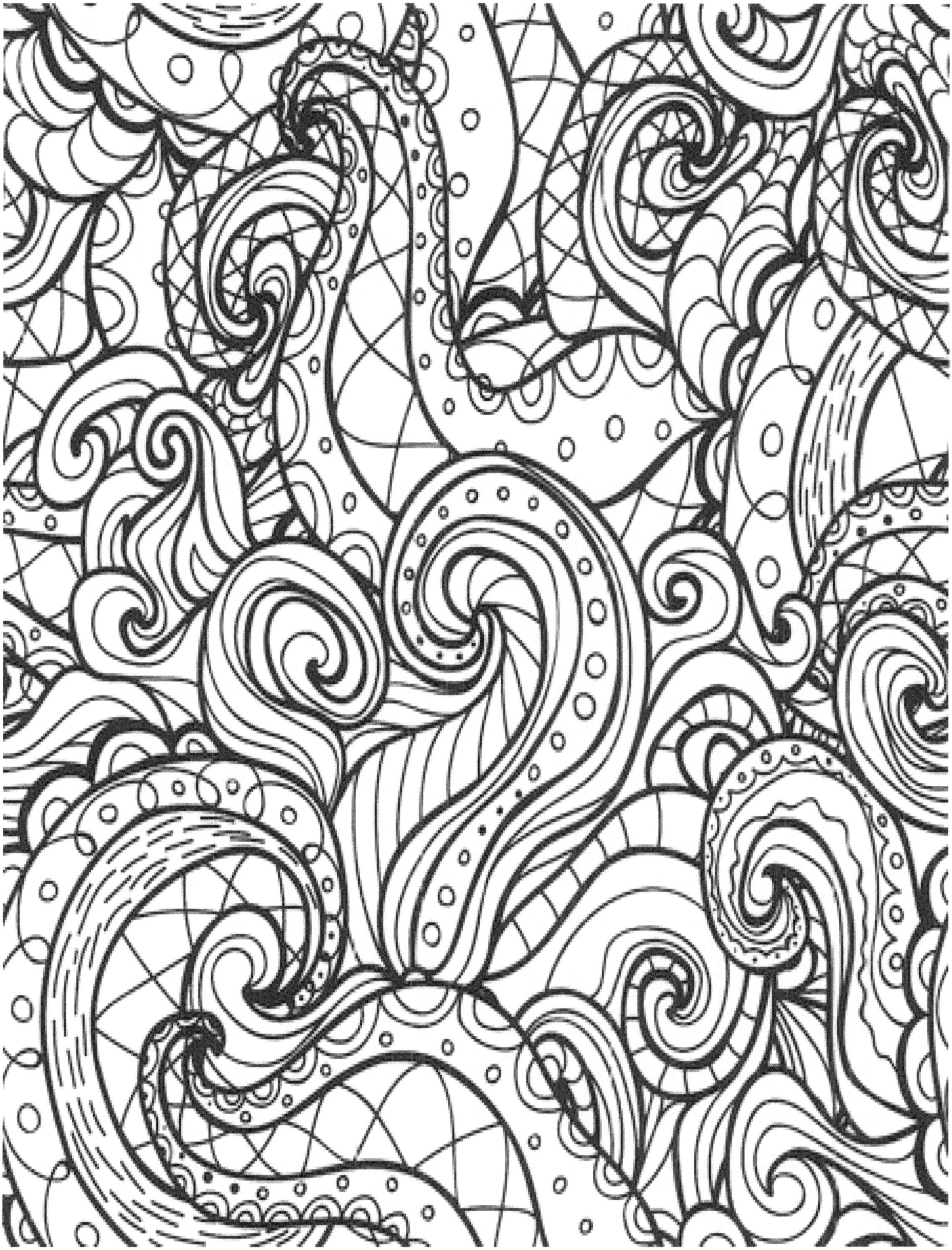

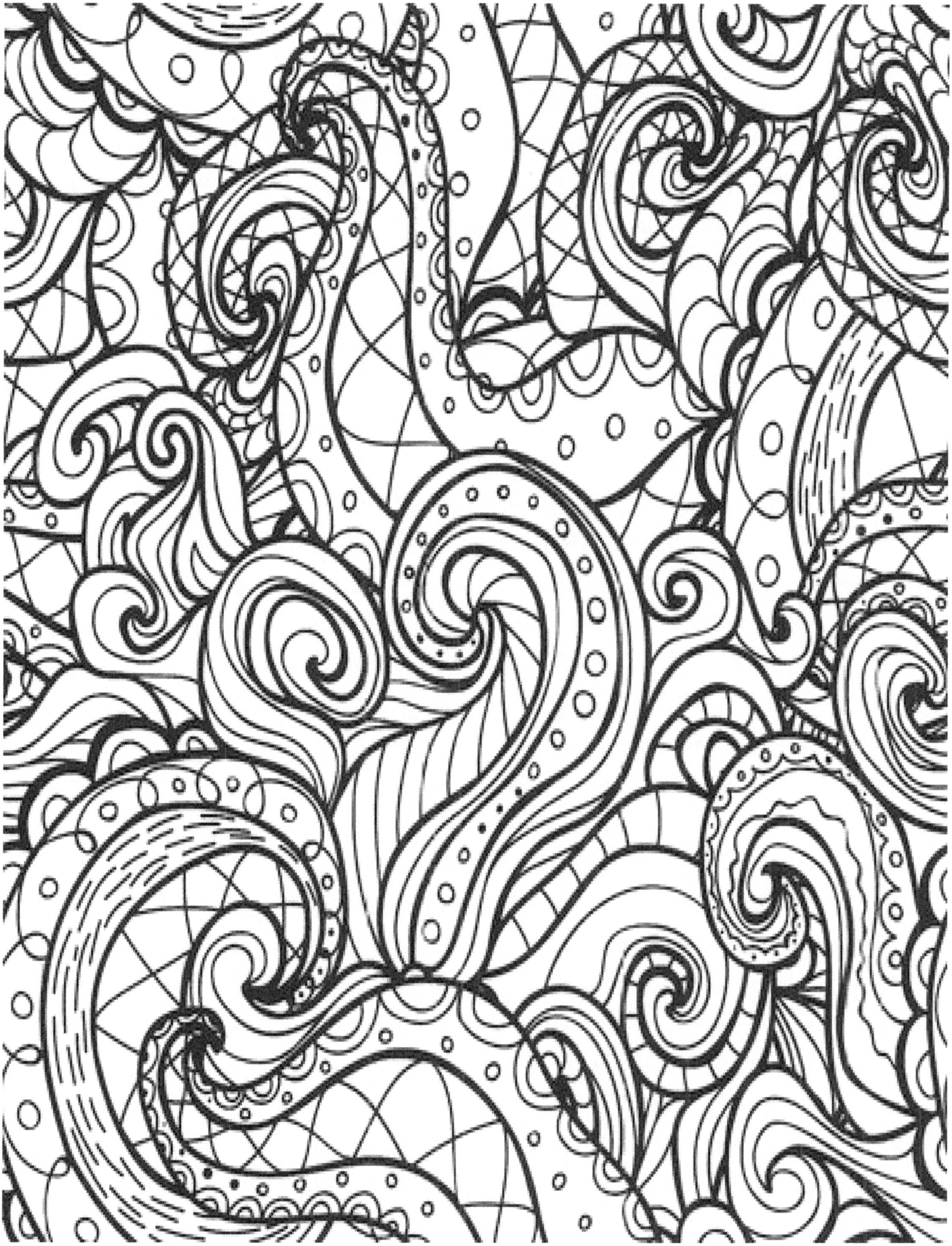

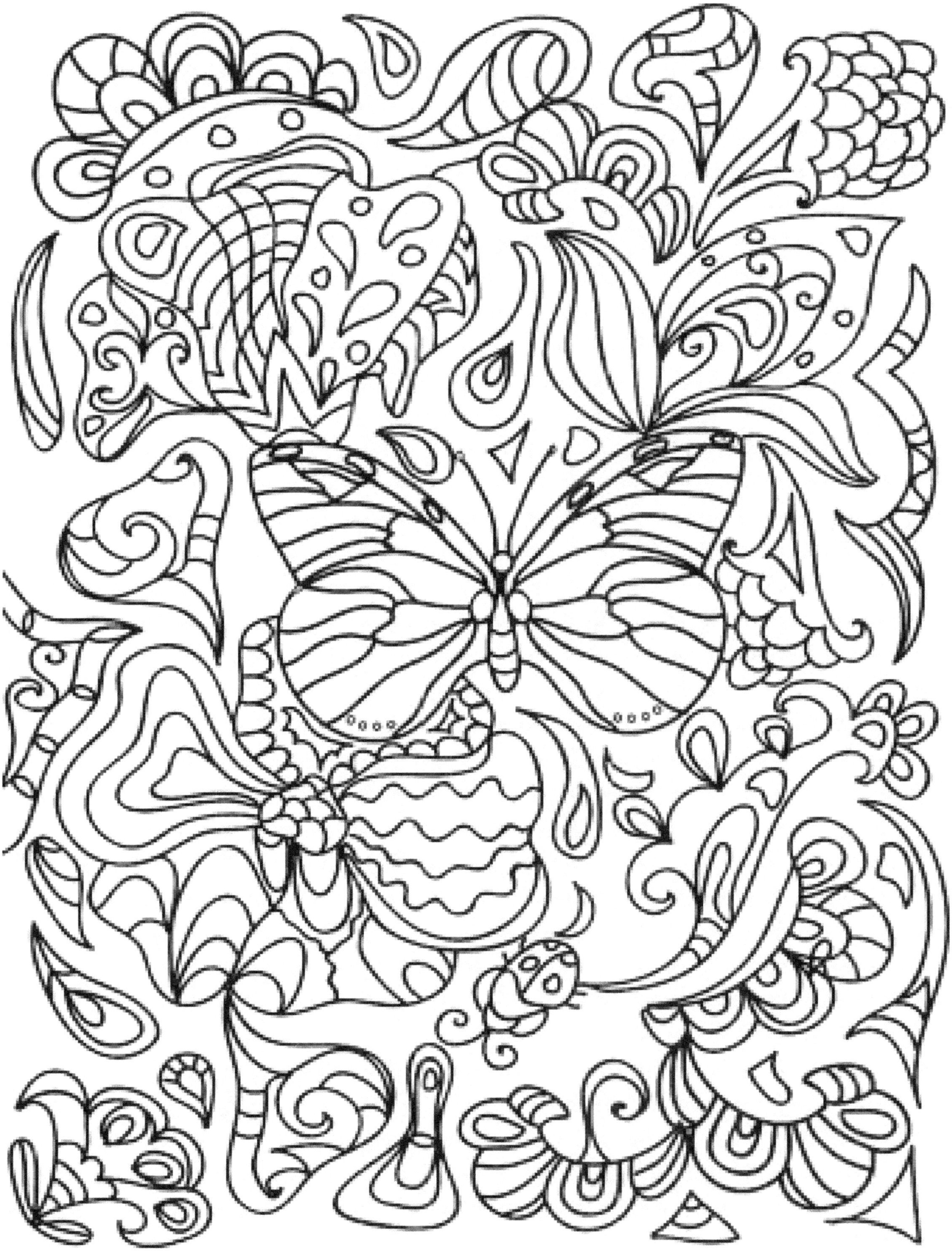

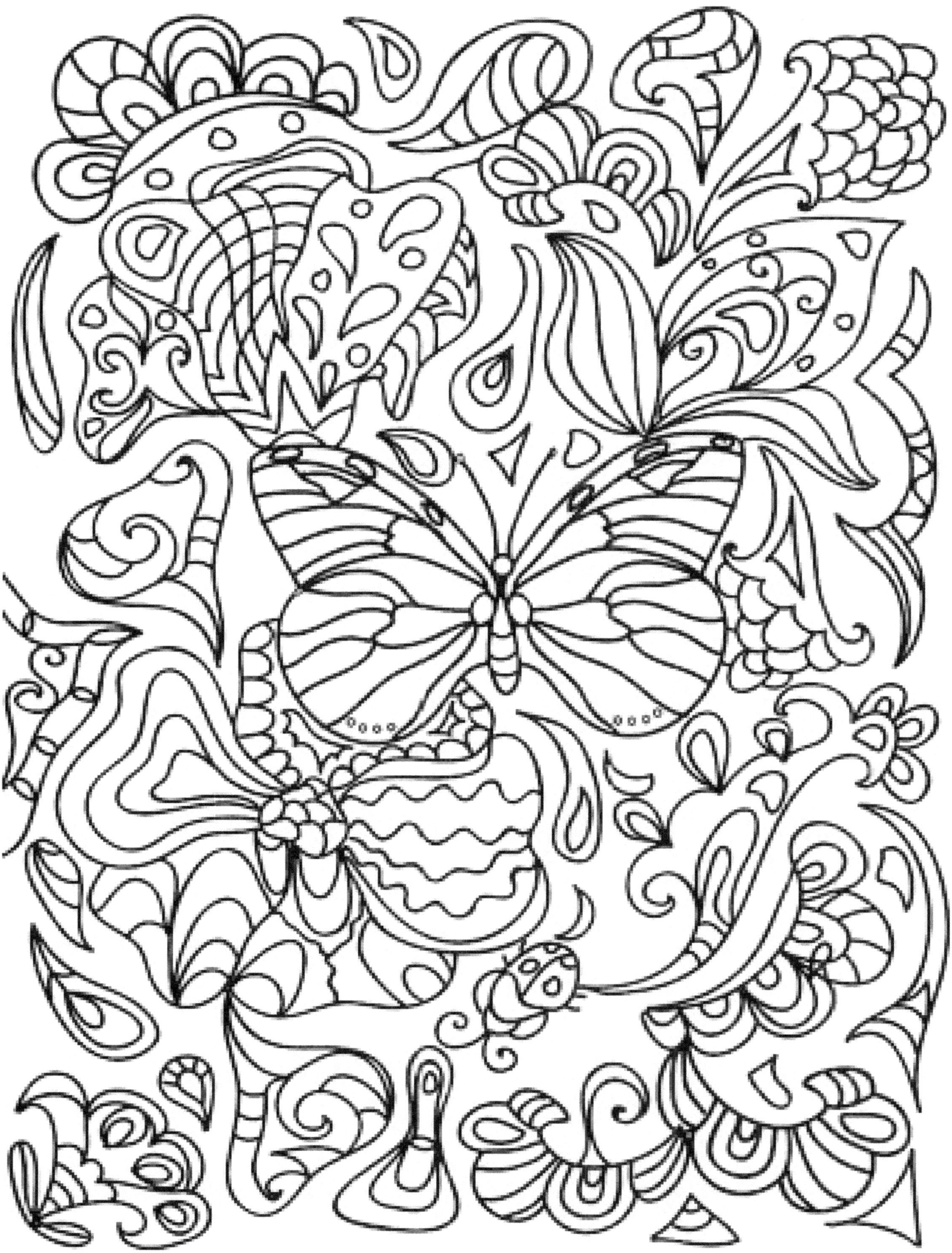

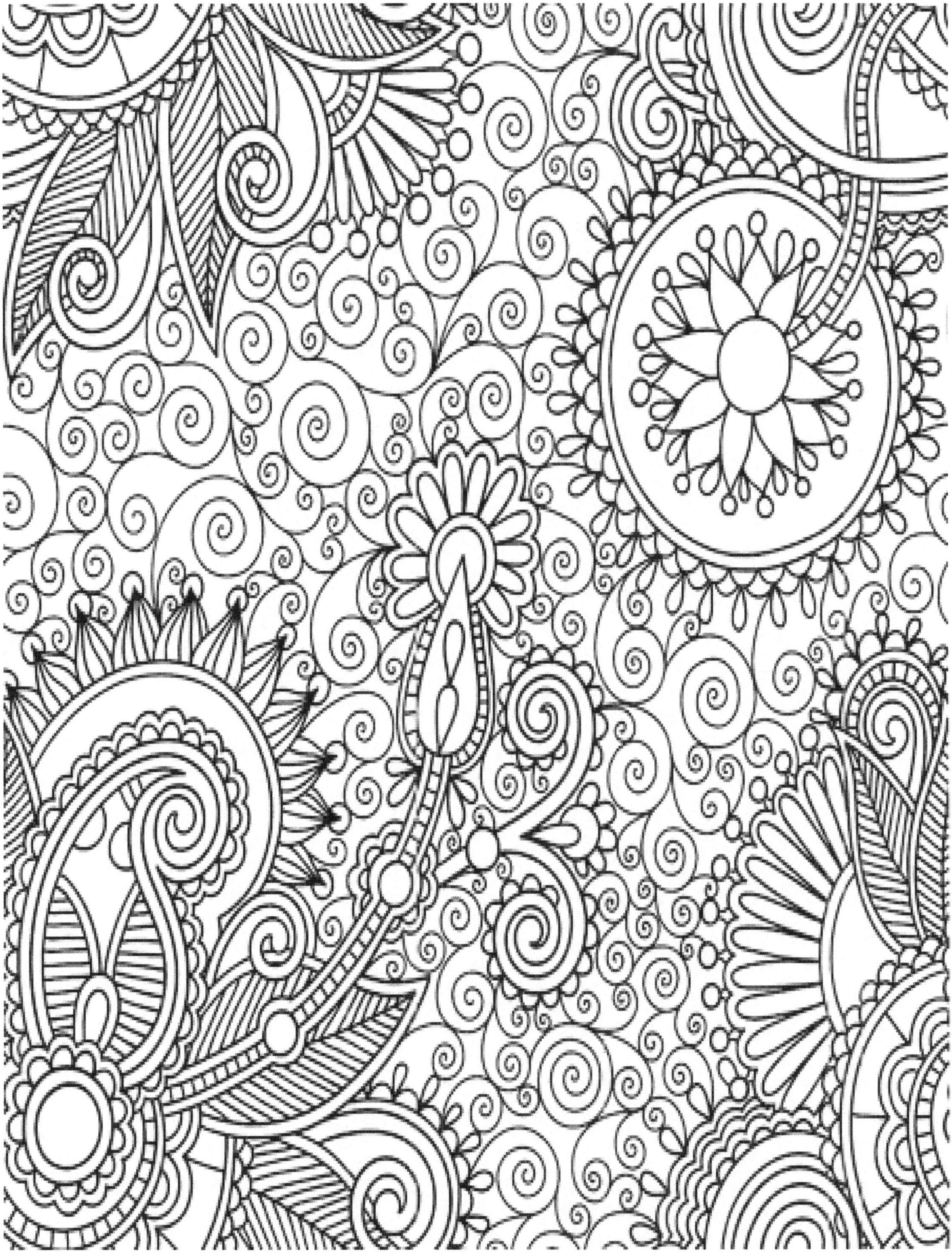

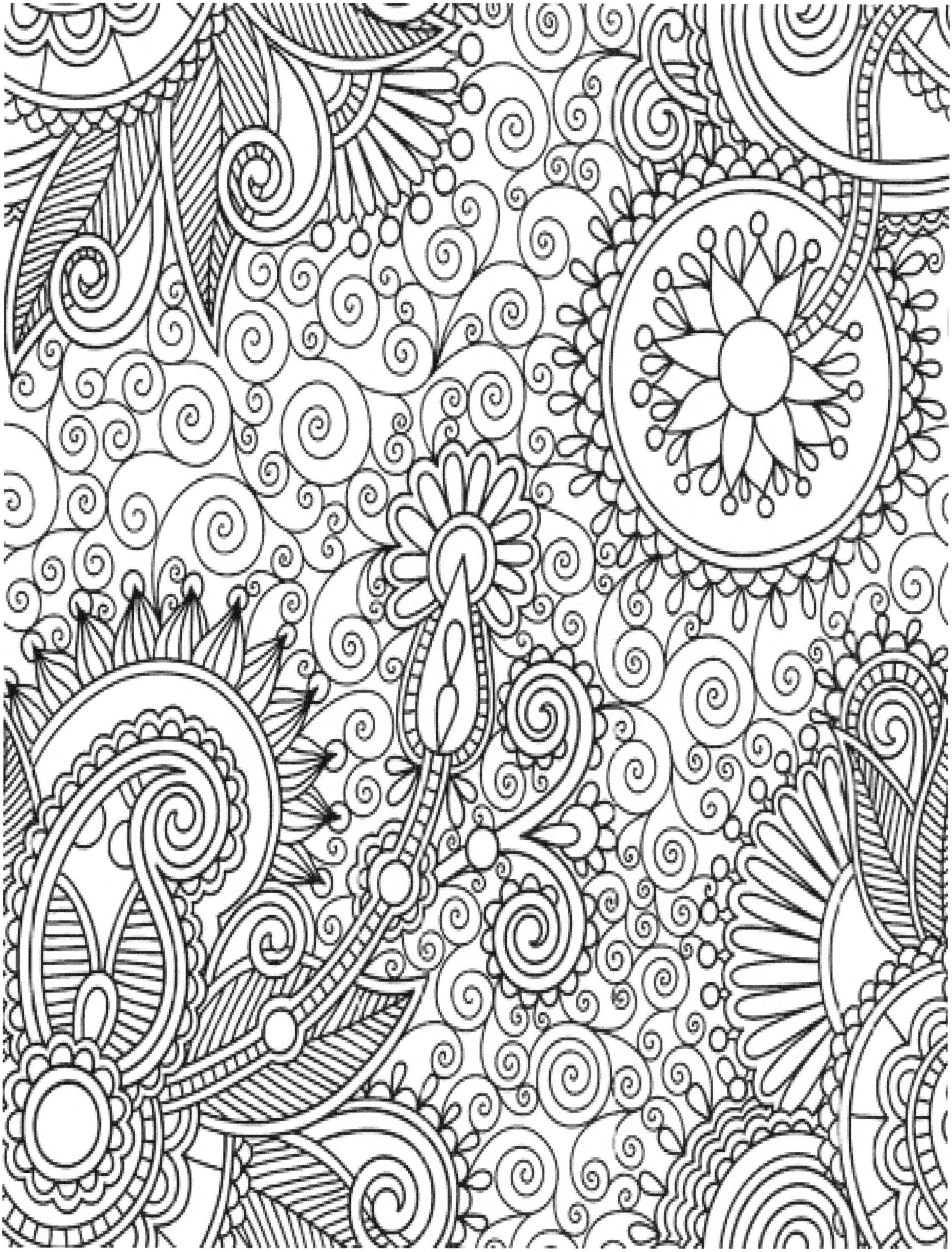

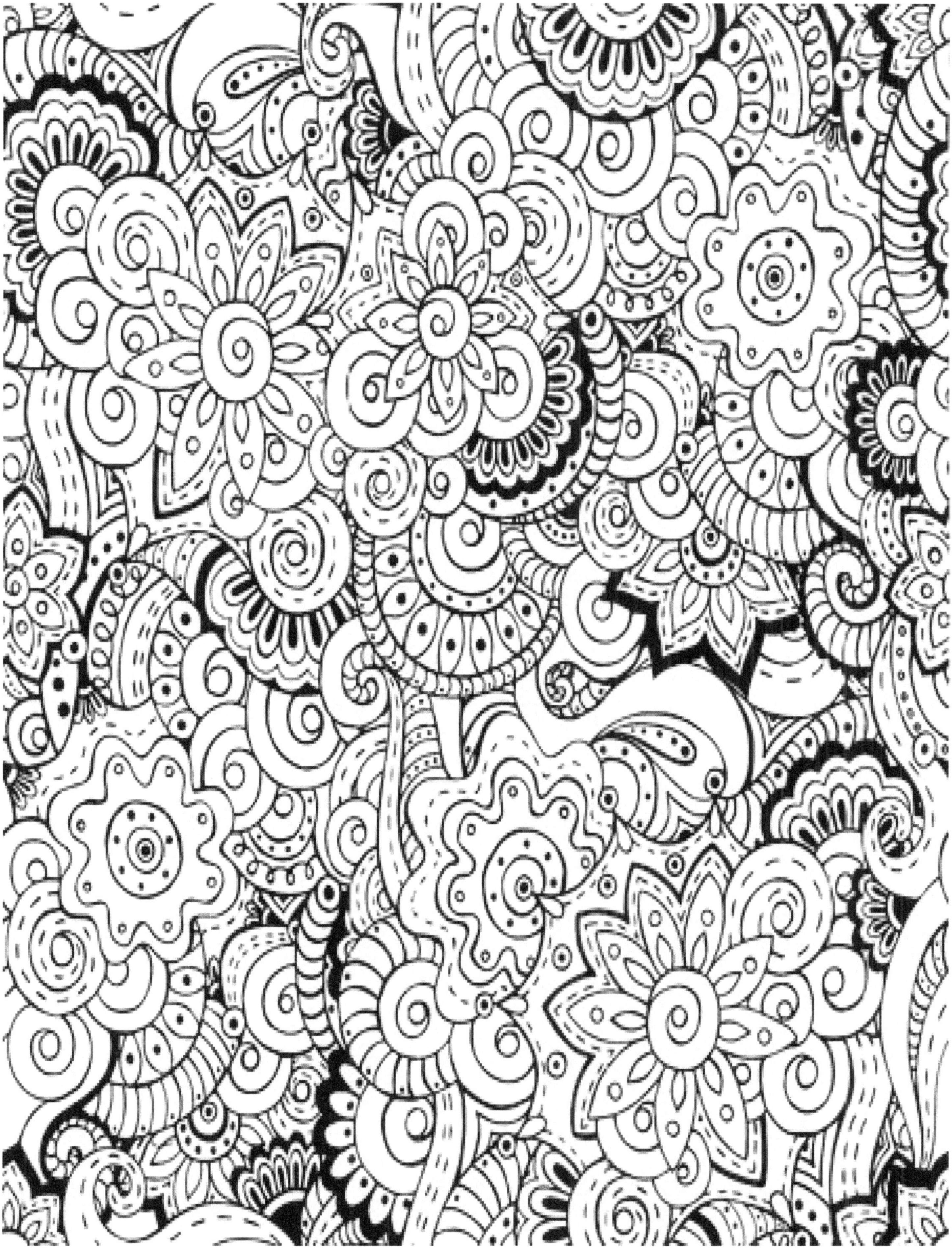

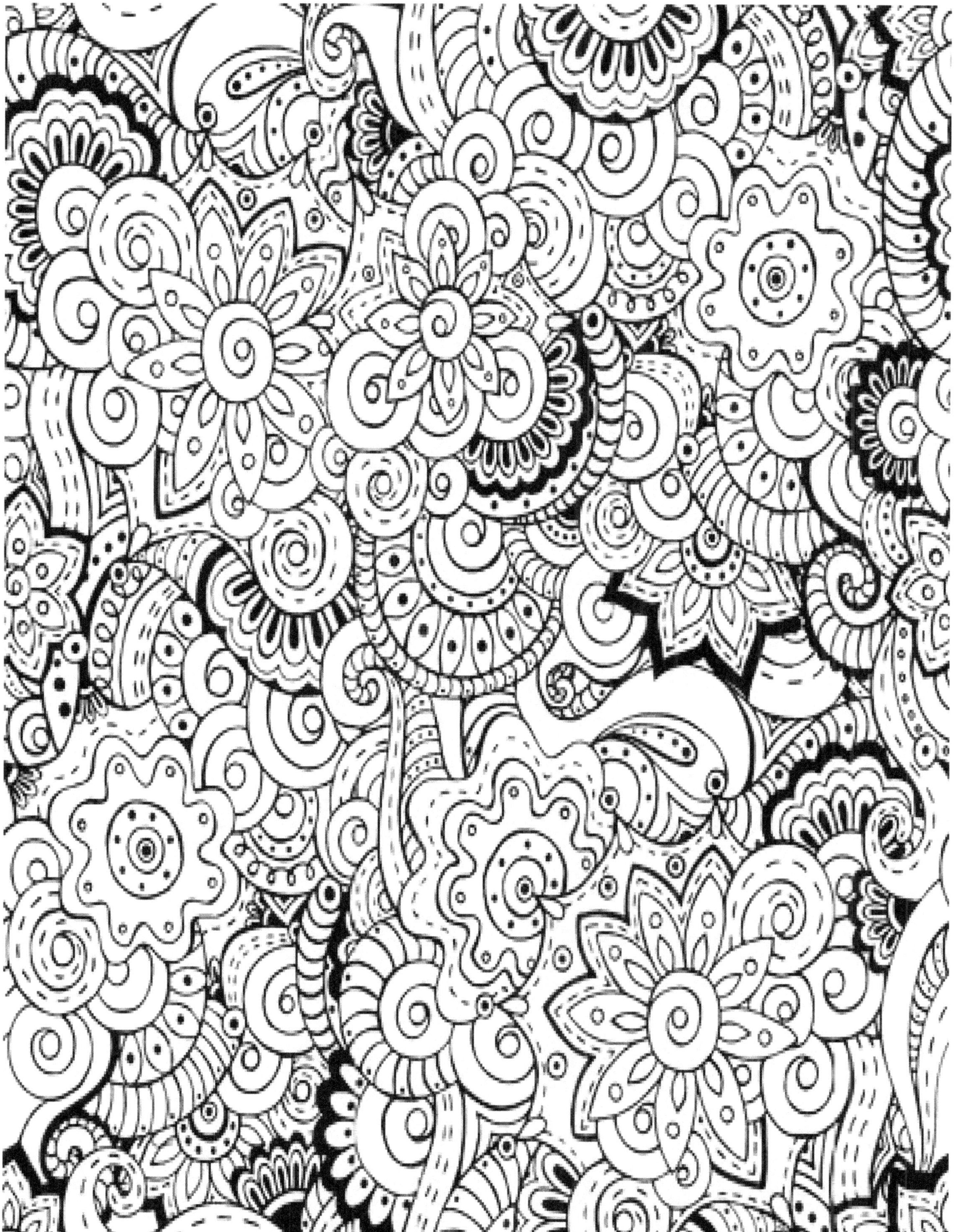

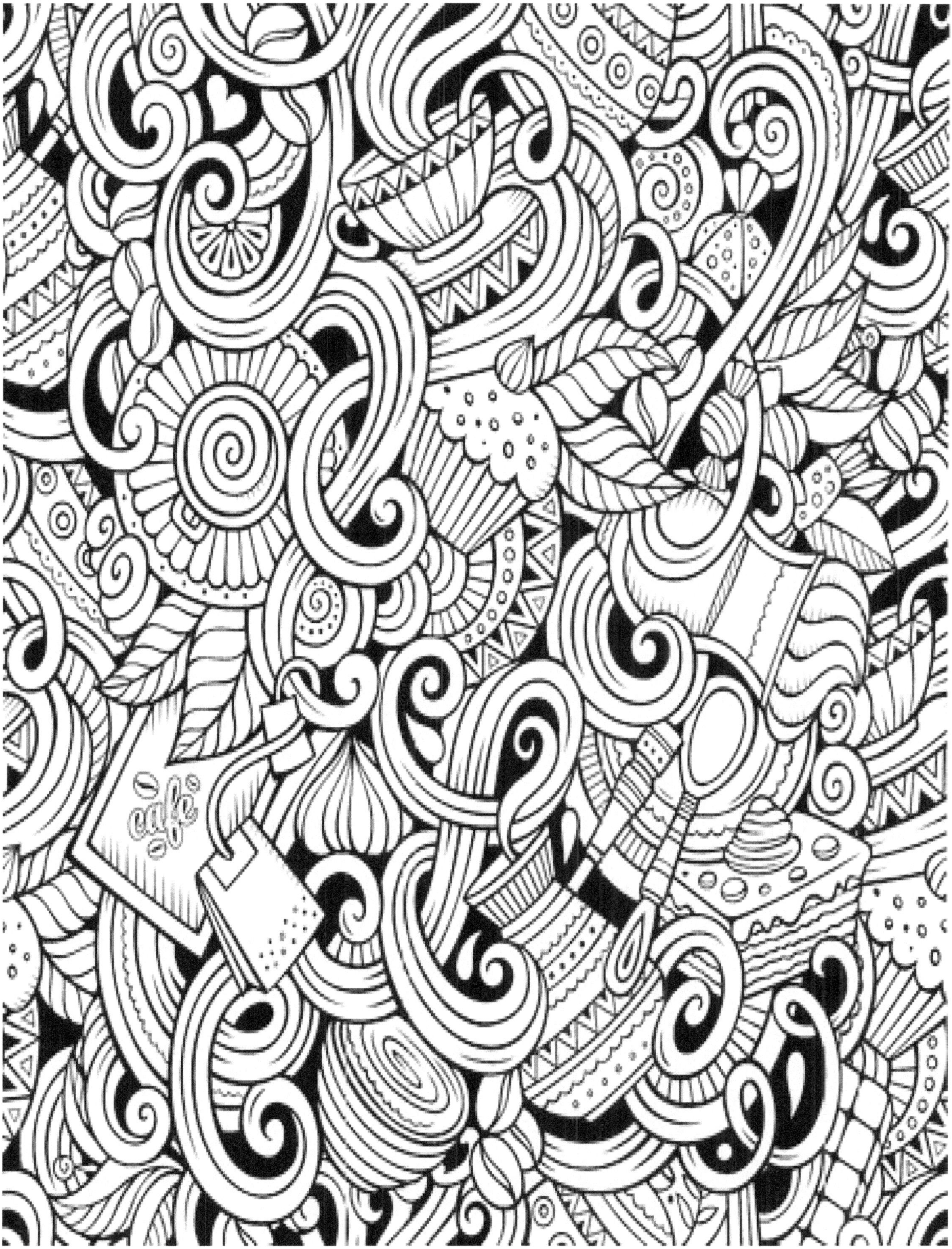
cafe

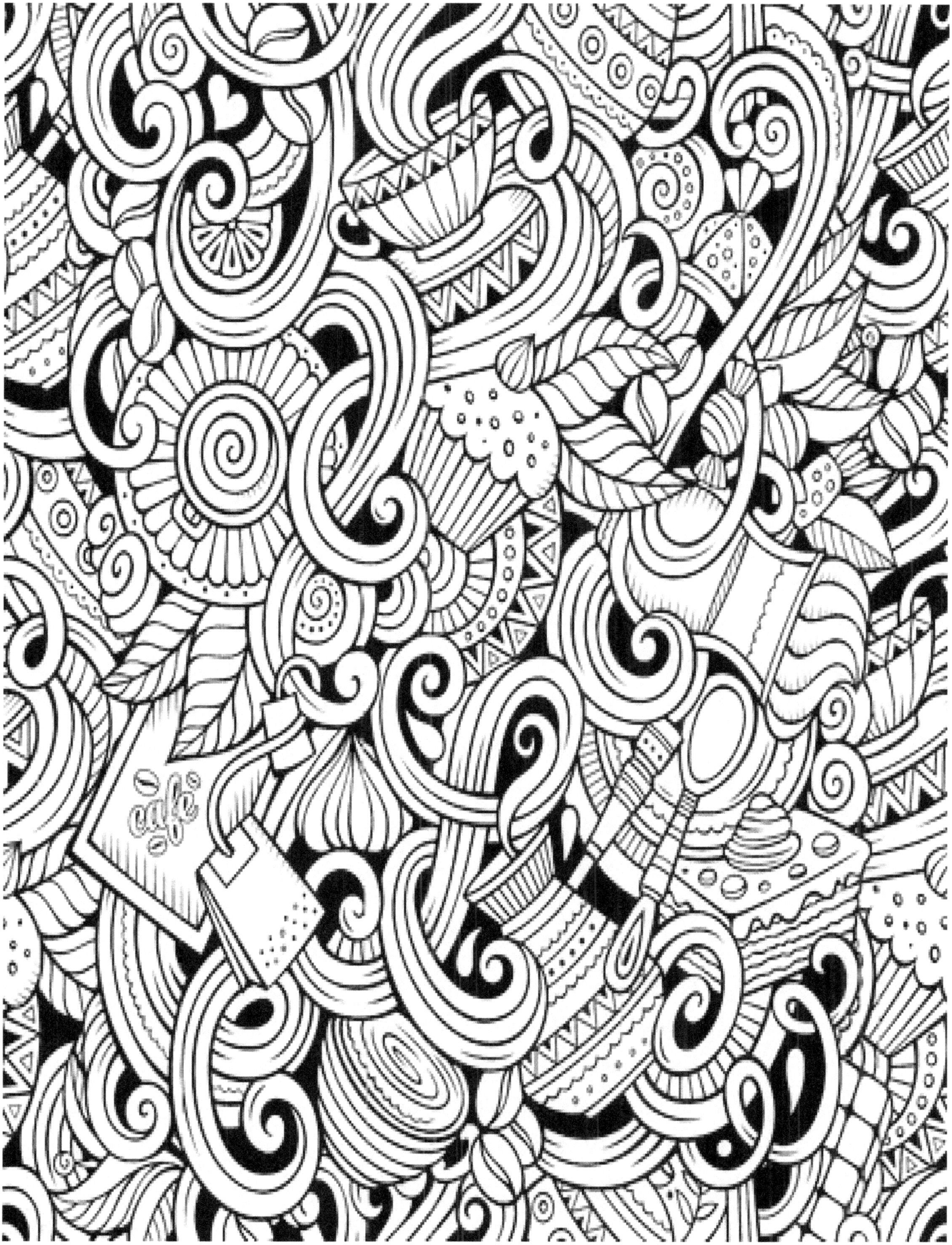
cafe

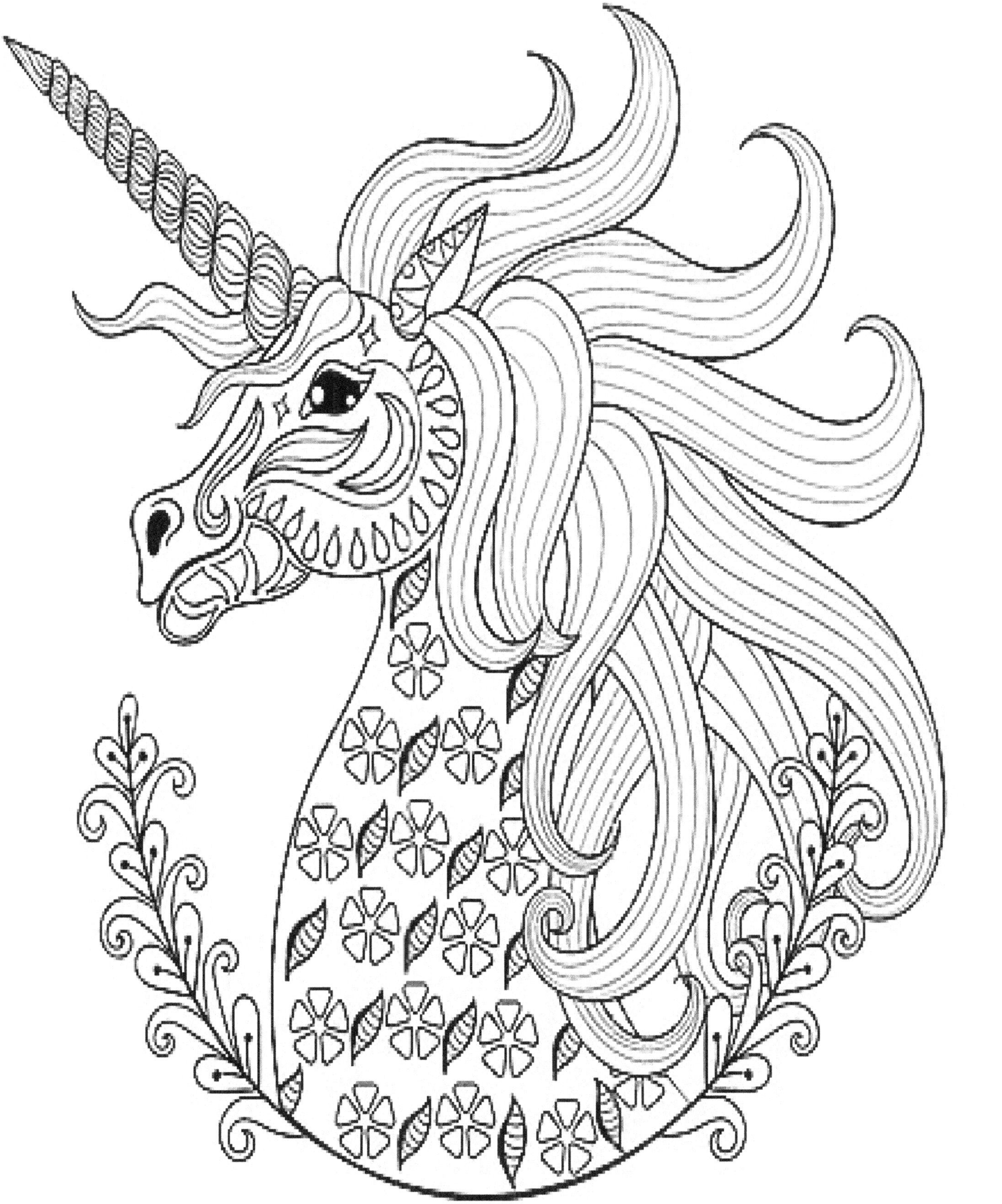

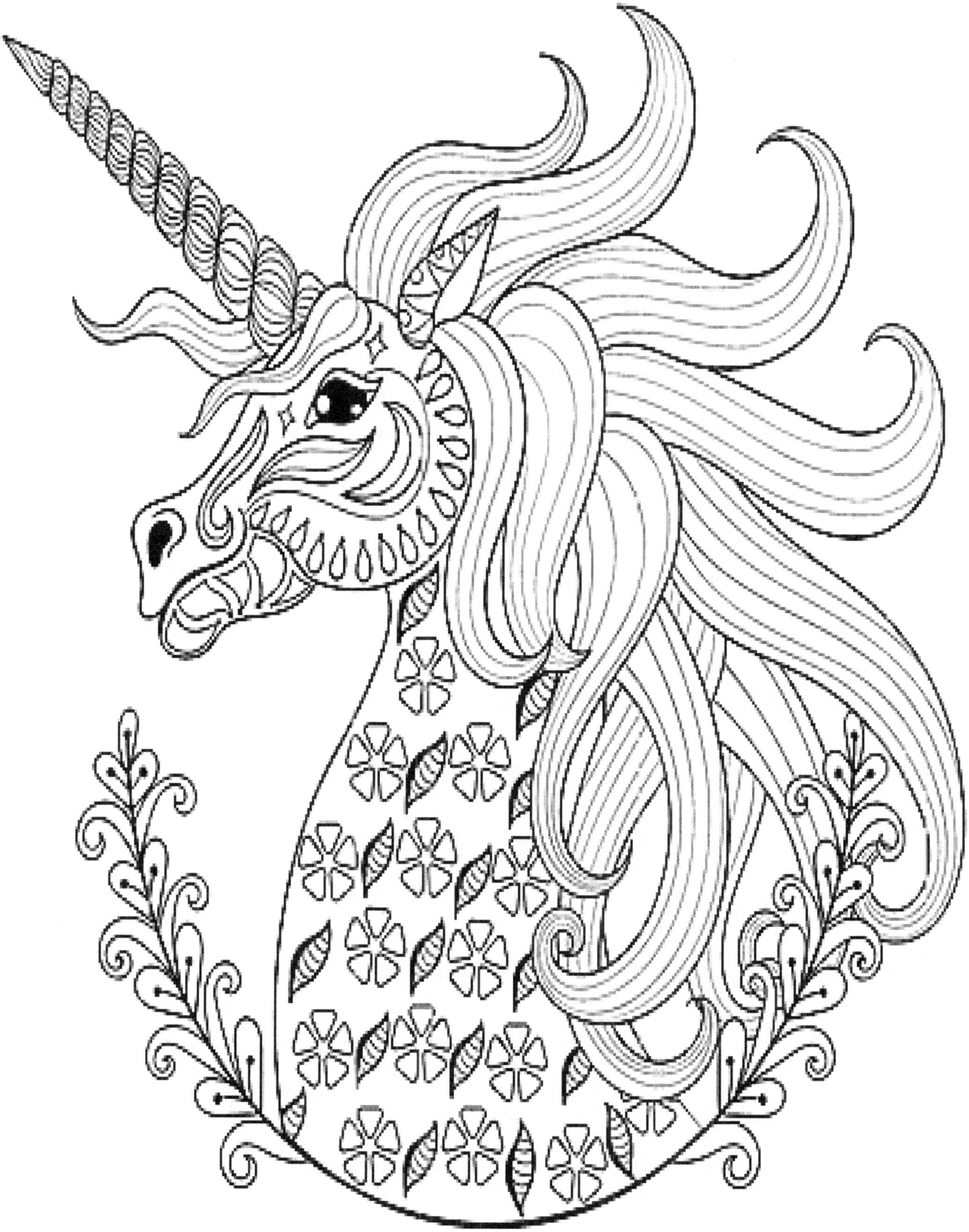

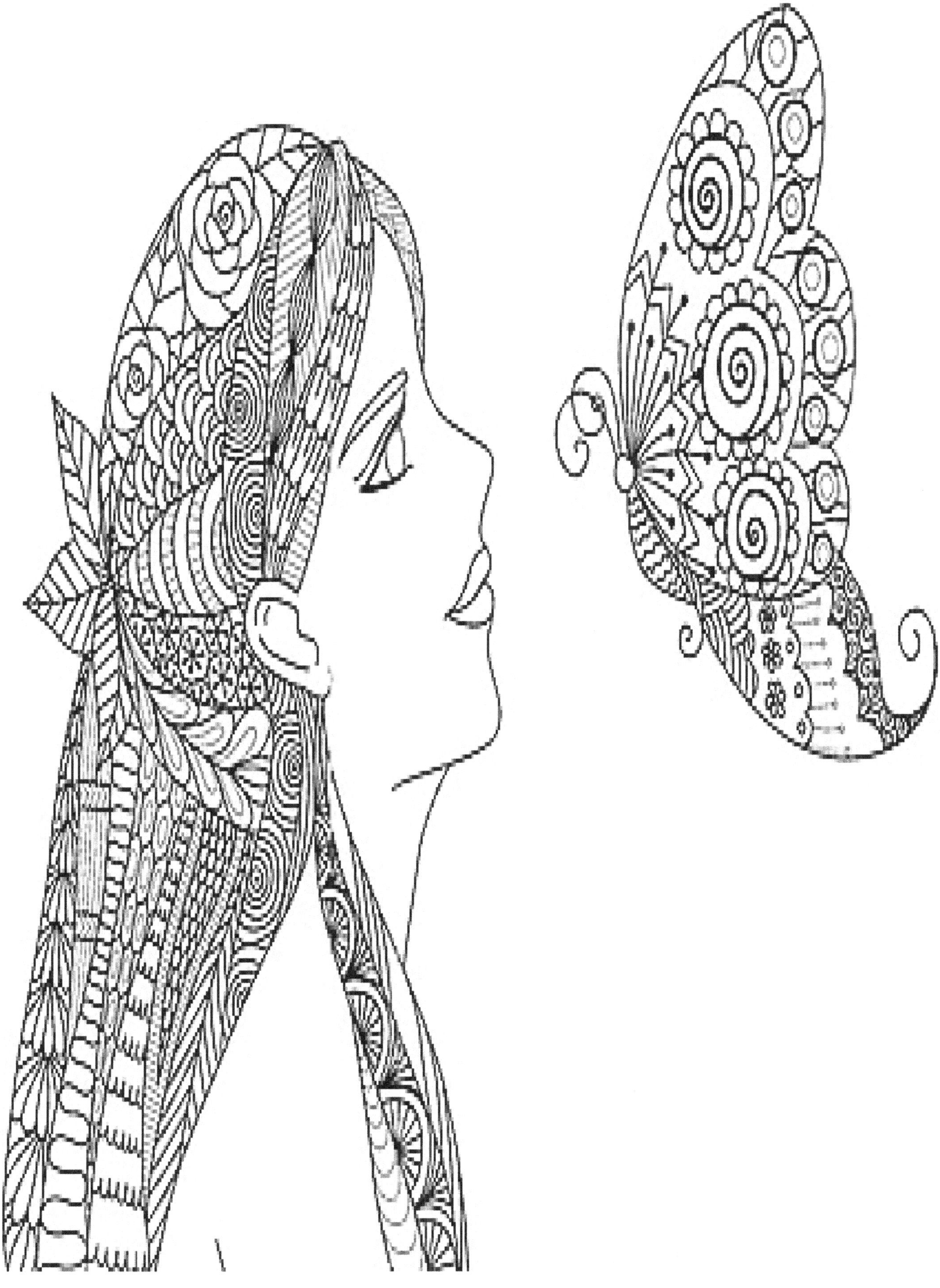

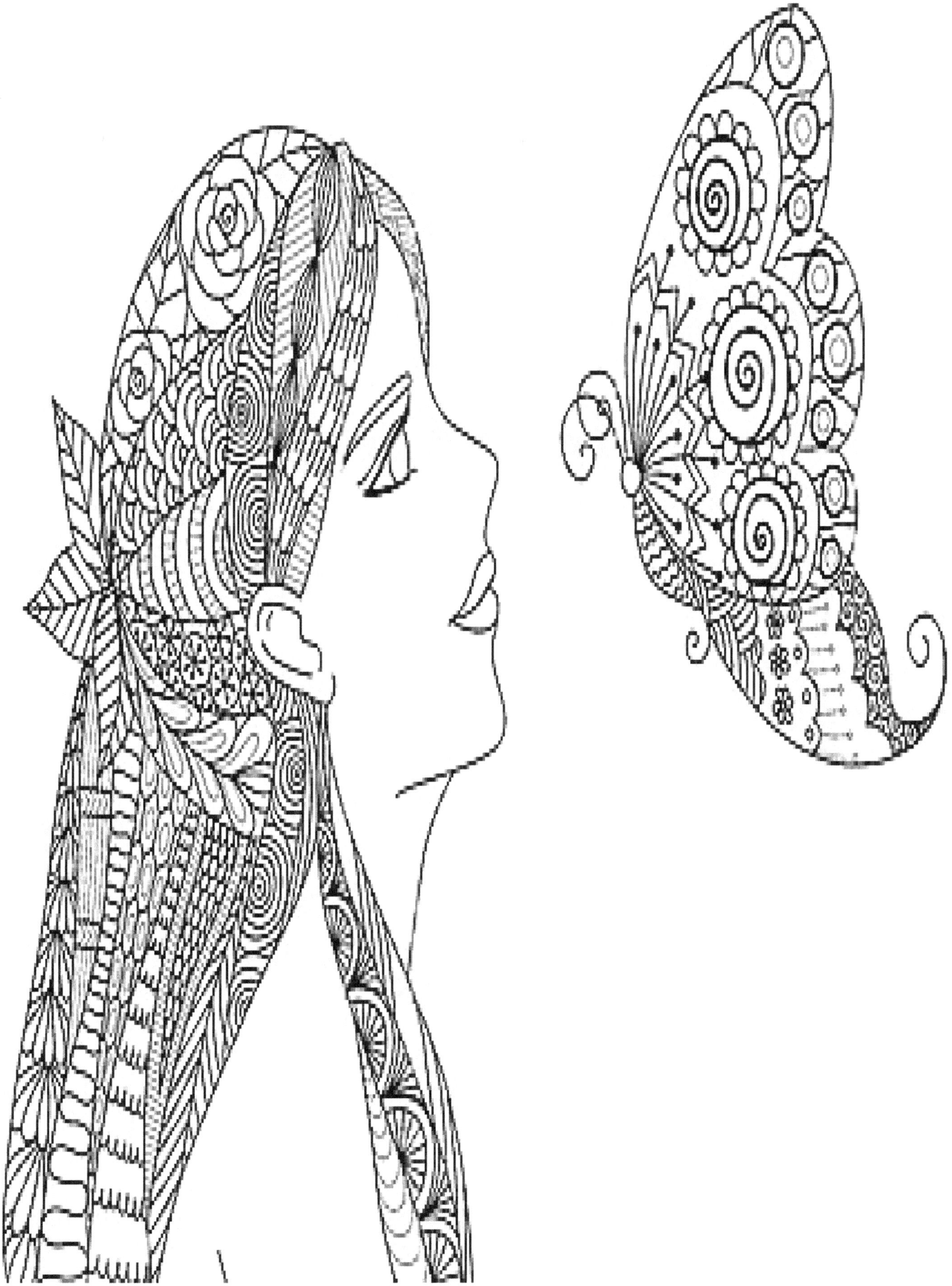

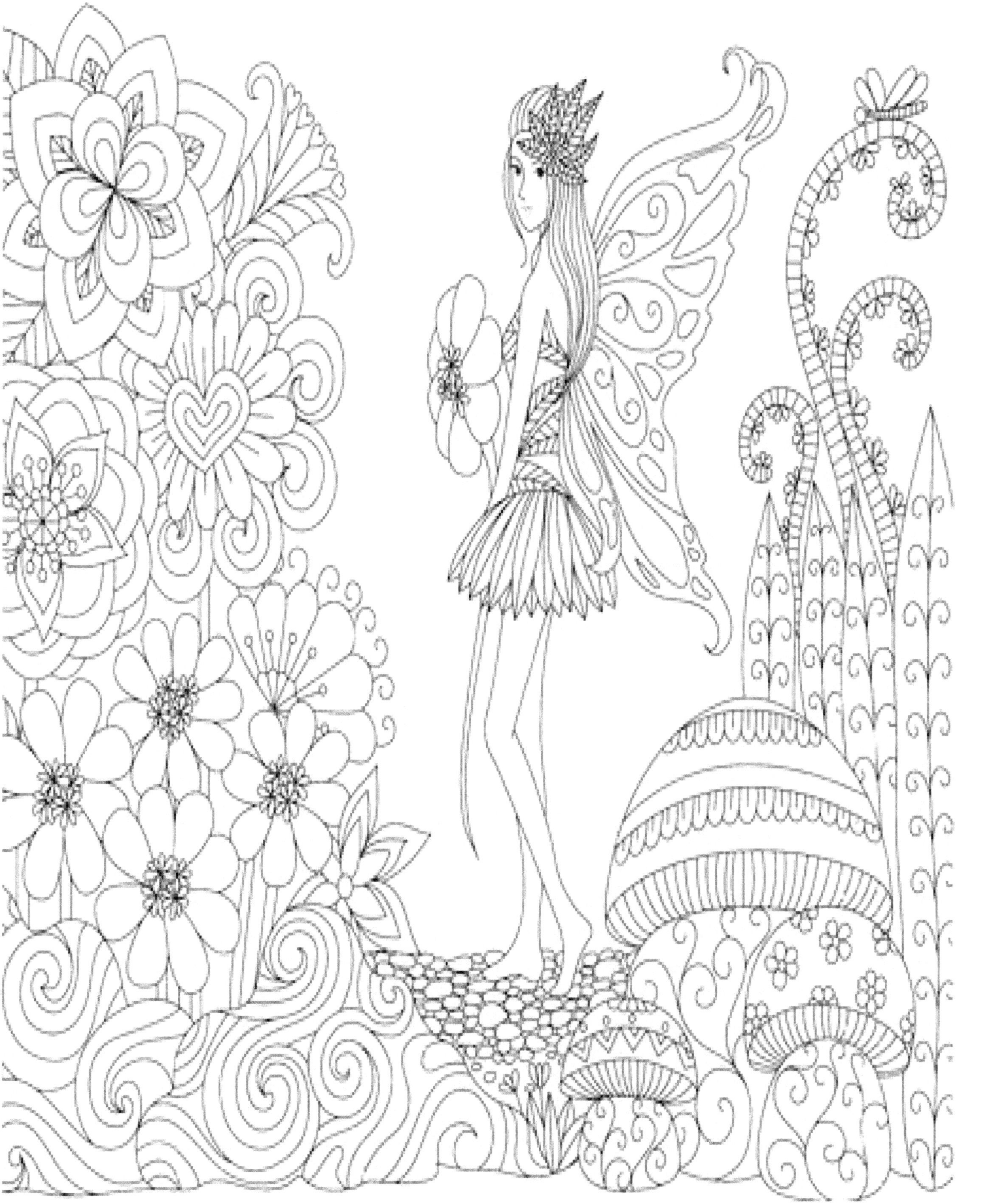

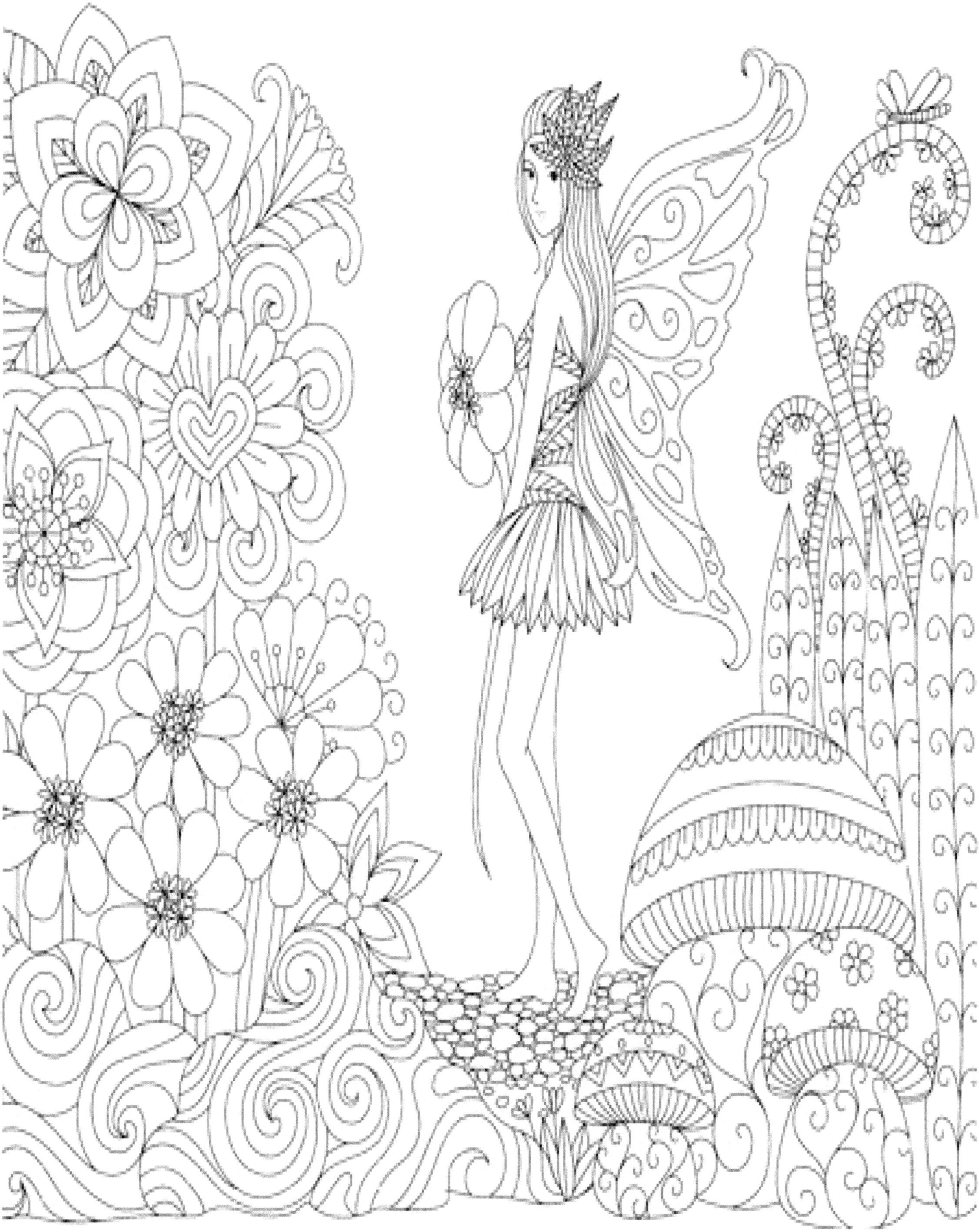

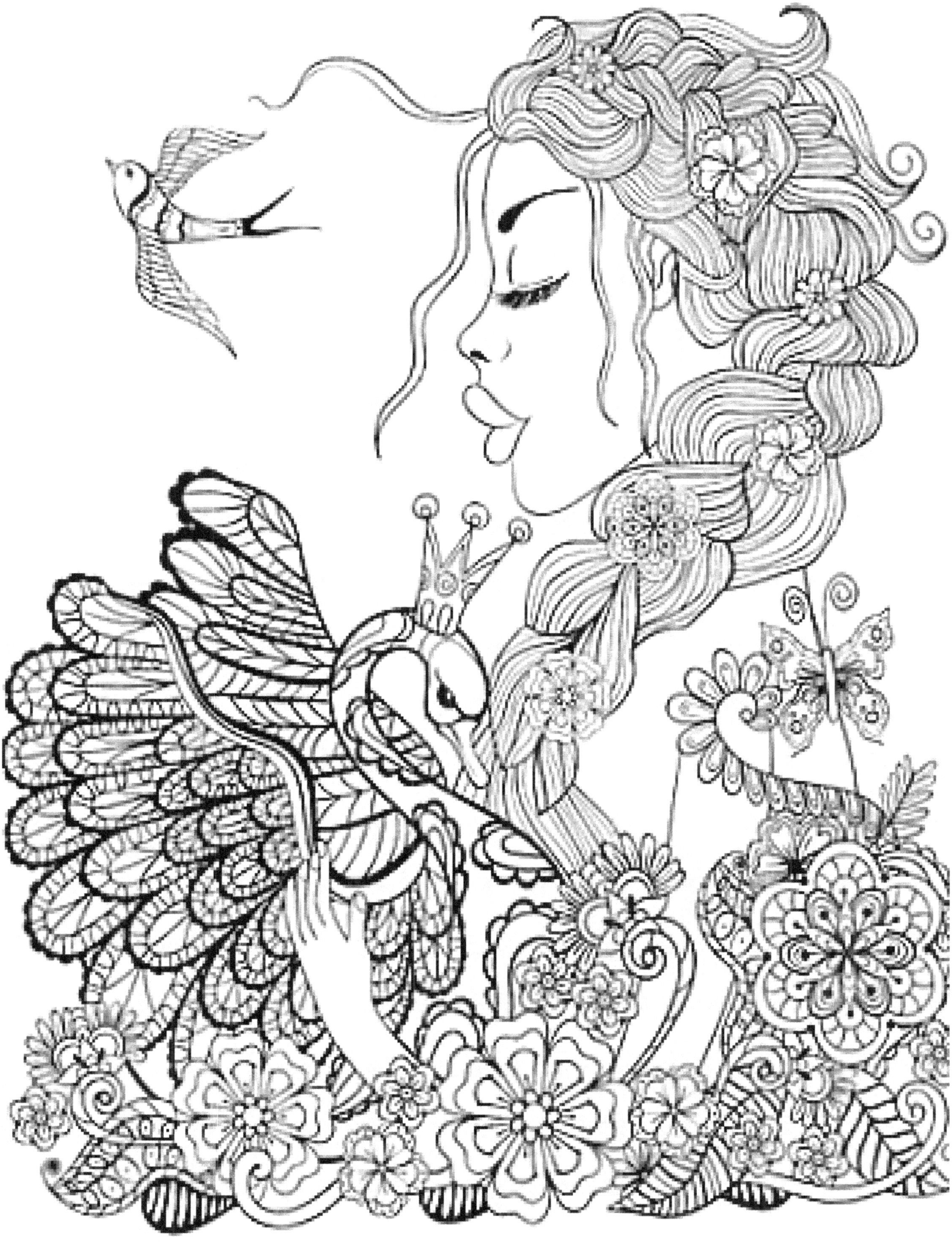

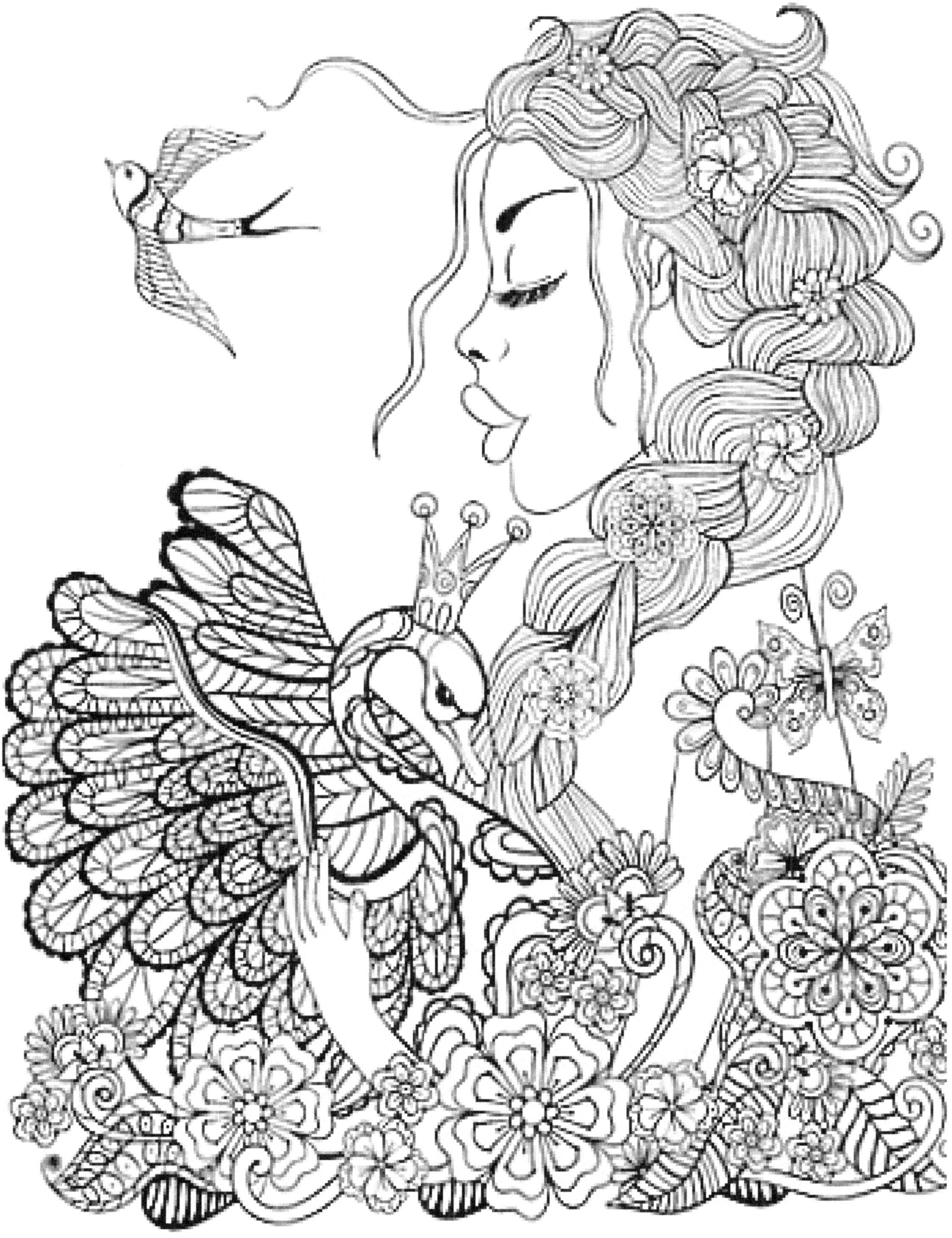

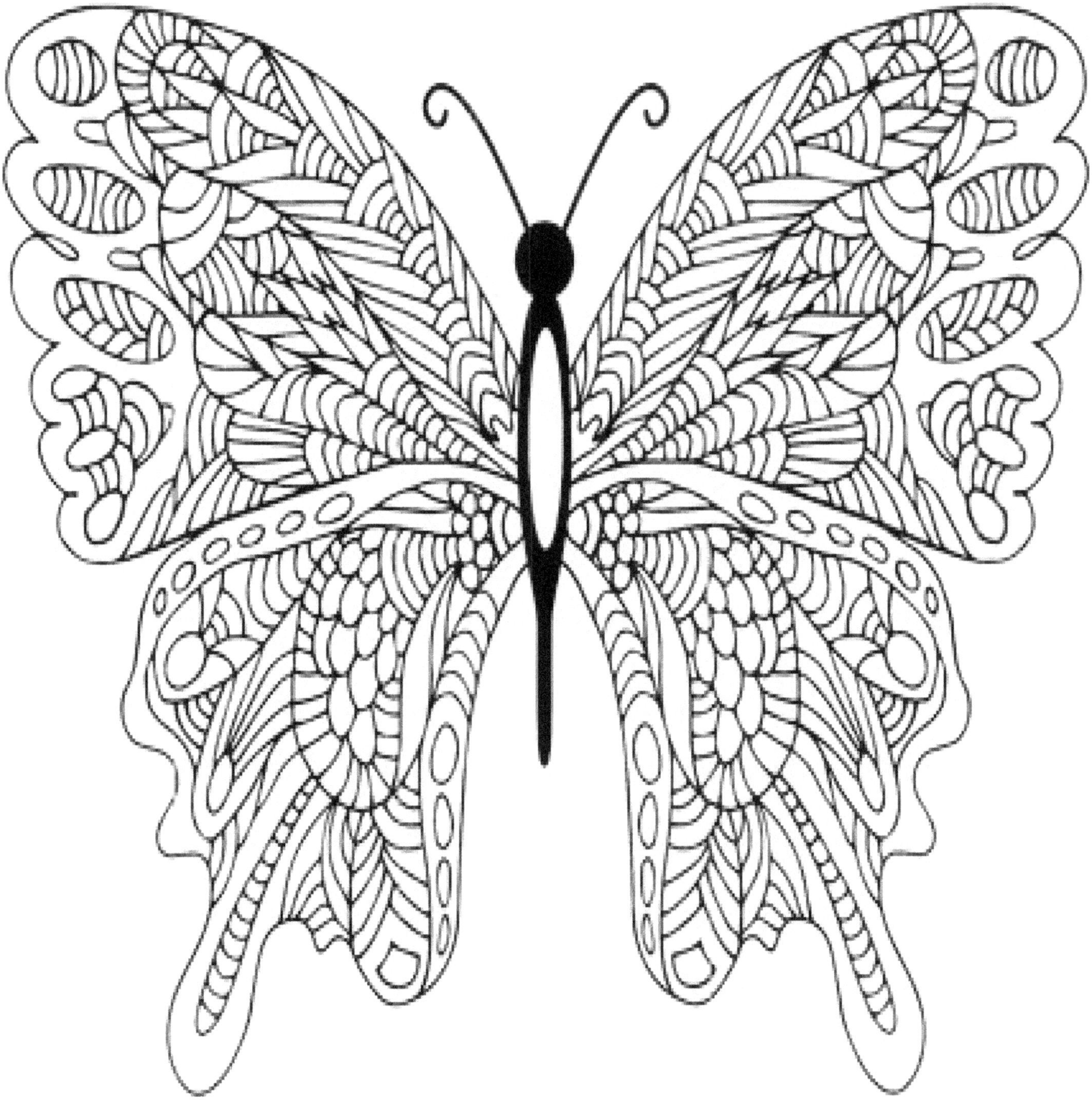

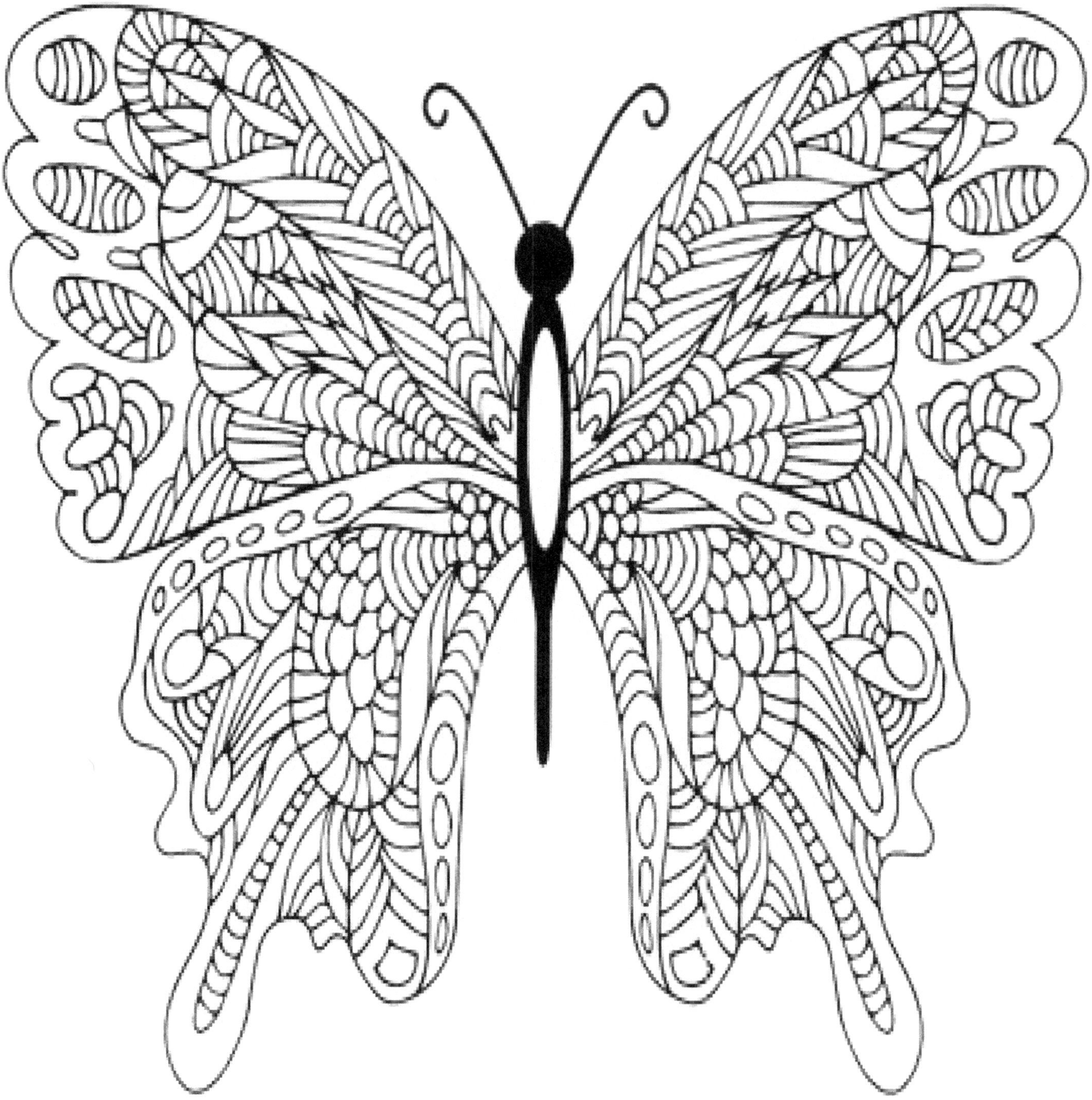

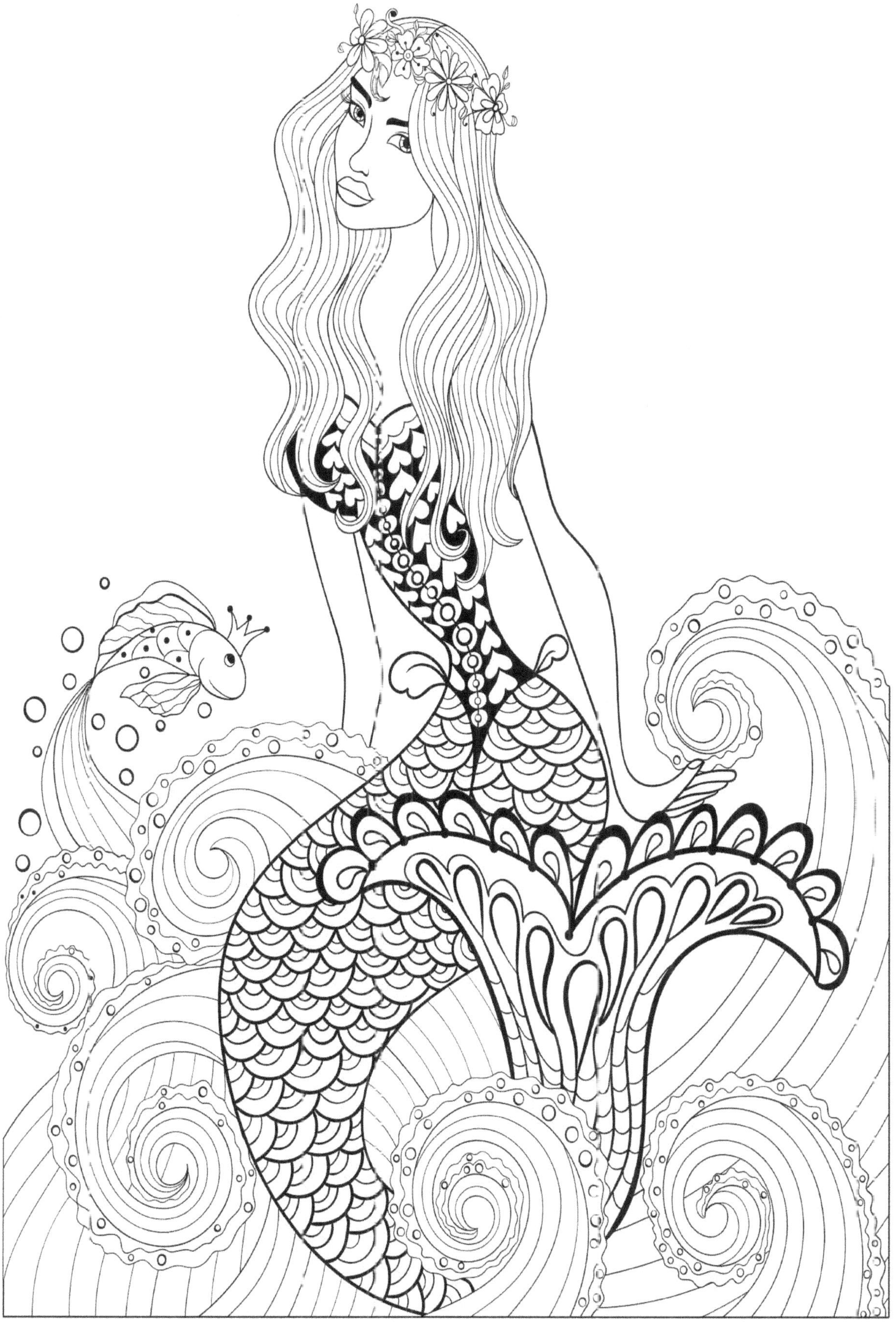

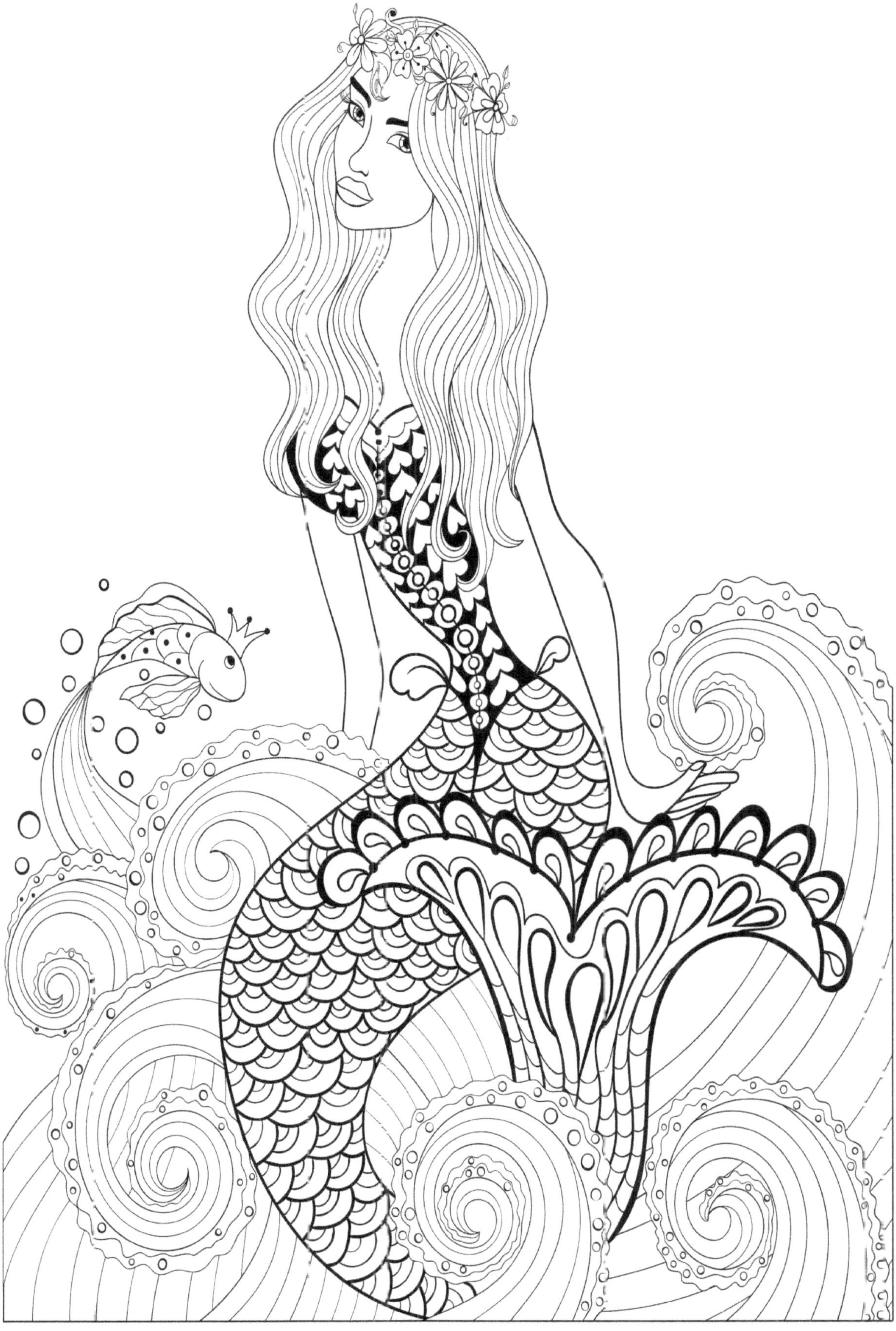

www.ingramcontent.com/pod-product-compliance
Lightning Source LLC
Chambersburg PA
CBHW080700190526
45169CB00006B/2193
* 9 7 8 1 5 3 0 4 7 2 5 2 9 *